LIGHT MIND

Mindfulness for Daily Living

To our children's grandparents, Lil Murphy and Arthur Morrin, Annie Finn and Luke Byrne.

LIGHT MIND

Mindfulness for Daily Living

With a special chapter for counsellors and
mental health workers

VERITAS

This edition published 2009 by
Veritas Publications
7–8 Lower Abbey Street
Dublin I, Ireland
Email publications@veritas.ie
Website www.veritas.ie

ISBN 978 1 84730 205 2
Copyright © Padraig O'Morain, 2009

10 9 8 7 6 5 4 3

A catalogue record for this book is available from the British
Library.

Printed in the Republic of Ireland by Gemini International,
Dublin

Veritas books are printed on paper made from the wood pulp of managed forests.
For every tree felled, at least one tree is planted, thereby renewing natural
resources.

Acknowledgements

Nyanaponika Thera's book, *The Heart of Buddhist Meditation*, introduced me to mindfulness one sunny afternoon in Dublin in 1992. Marcella Finnerty and Norah Byrne encouraged me to introduce mindfulness to counselling students at the Institute of Integrative Counselling and Psychotherapy in Tallaght, Dublin. Conversations with fellow counsellor and practitioner Breda McGee have deepened my understanding of mindfulness. Though we have not yet met in person, Gregg Krech and Linda Anderson Krech, through their work for the ToDo Institute in Vermont, have enhanced my awareness of mindfulness in daily life. Ruth Kennedy of Veritas gave me the opportunity to write this book and Catherine Gough was a wise and sensitive editor. I am grateful to all.

A First Mindfulness Practice

What's happening around you right now?
What do you hear?
What do you see?
How do your clothes feel against your body?
How are you breathing: long breath, short breath, rough, smooth?
As you answer these questions you are practising mindfulness.

Simple? Yes.

But in a few minutes, perhaps in a few seconds, your mind will have drifted into a memory or a fantasy.

So, not that simple.

Read on ...

CONTENTS

A Word on Mindfulness Exercises   13

Introductions and Explanations

Mindfulness? What's that?   15
A note on history   16
Mindfulness is a practice – always   17
A basic mindfulness exercise   18
Acceptance – the heart of mindfulness   20
Non-judgemental awareness   22
Kindness   26
A kindness meditation   28
Euphoria warning   29
Pleasant, unpleasant, neutral   30

The Moment

Impermanence   33
What quality am I bringing to this moment?   34
What is this? Returning again and again to mindfulness   35
What am I doing here? Mindfulness of intention   37
Wakening up from the trance   38
Habit energy – how routine can make life stale   41
Associations and tags – when labels take over reality   43

Hustle and Bustle

Cues – calling back the wandering mind   47
The Lake – a practice in broad awareness   48
Patience – a side-effect of mindfulness   50
Bully at work   51
How mindfulness makes for better planning   53

Body and Mind

Breathing – a foundation of mindfulness practice 57
Body scan 60
Walking as a mindfulness practice 61
Touch – always here and now 62
Three benefits of mindful eating 63
Notice the light 65
Mindfulness of sound 66
Standing 68
Increase your pleasure through awareness 70
The hedonic treadmill, a.k.a. 'the grass is always greener on the other side' 72
Loosening the bonds 75
Mindful stillness 77

Stress and Distress

How mindfulness improves your chances of a good night's sleep 79
Panic attacks 81
Living with emotional pain 83
Staying out of the drama – mindfulness and anger 85
Allowing resentment to blow away 87
Anxiety and the mindfulness path of acceptance 90
Depression 92
Recession – living through anxious times 98
From the cellar – memory and mindfulness 100
Two kinds of suffering: primary and secondary 103
Chronic pain and mindfulness 105
Deep injustice 107

Encounters

What about me? Mindfulness, the self and
relationships   112
Relationships and mindfulness – keeping a fresh,
authentic view   114
Parenting   115
Spirituality and mindfulness   117

Mindfulness in Sports

Mindfulness: essential sports equipment   120

Mindfulness in Counselling, Psychotherapy and Mental Health Settings

A case study   124
Definition and explanation   125
A basic mindfulness exercise   126
Background to mindfulness practice   127
Practice and research   129
A note of caution   133
Further exercises   135

Sources and references for counsellors, psychotherapists
and other mental health workers   137

Notes   139

Appendix: The Quick Guide to Mindfulness   141

A WORD ON MINDFULNESS
EXERCISES

In this book I want to encourage you to practise mindfulness in your daily life and to show you how to do it. That is why the book mingles explanations of the uses of mindfulness with specific mindfulness exercises.

Mindfulness looks simple – just cultivate a deliberate awareness of what is happening for you in the present moment. But the mind wanders into fantasy and memory again and again. Therefore, we need ways to anchor ourselves to the here and now. The many mindfulness exercises in this book will help you to do that. All can be completed relatively quickly. You can use your exercises several times a day. These will connect you with your here-and-now experience. When you make such a connection, with a non-judgemental and kind attitude, you practise mindfulness.

People who are deeply 'into' mindfulness might do one of these exercises for forty minutes to an hour every day, but this book is about what I call 'light mindfulness', so I am not recommending practices of that length. For most of us, the chances that we will stick to a forty-minutes-a-day regime are remote. Moreover, lengthy meditation practices are best undertaken, in my view, as part of a course or meditation group, or in conjunction with a mentor or counsellor. This is because lengthy meditations can bring up material, such as memories that have been long forgotten or repressed, which can be disturbing. Sometimes it is good to recover repressed memories, but that is a challenging process best undertaken, as I have said, in conjunction with a mentor or counsellor.

For the practice of light mindfulness you might use these exercises briefly, several times a day. If you can put time aside, you may choose to spend ten minutes or so a day on a favourite exercise. If you can do so, you will greatly improve the quality of your mindfulness practice. If not, then find some exercises in this book to do briefly, perhaps in the morning and at night and once or twice during the day. This will make a difference.

INTRODUCTIONS AND EXPLANATIONS

Mindfulness? What's that?

Mindfulness is awareness of the present moment, but that's not all.

Mindfulness is living in the here and now, but that's not all.

Mindfulness is knowing what you're doing when you're doing it, but that's not all.

Mindfulness is all these things, yes, but it is also acceptance, curiosity, a non-judgemental attitude towards your experience and, perhaps the really difficult part, an attitude of kindness towards yourself.

Here is a description of the mechanics of mindfulness:
Take your attention away from the past and future and away from your imagination. Become aware of what is going on right now. Notice with your senses: what you are seeing and hearing; that you are breathing; standing; walking or sitting or lying down; the feel of the air against your skin as you move along. Your mind will keep drifting out of the present so you need to keep bringing it back. *It is bringing your mind back to the present that makes up the basic practice of mindfulness.*

Note that I said the 'basic' practice of mindfulness. You could become aware of what is going on for you in the here and now and you could judge yourself very harshly for feeling whatever it is you notice you are feeling. But mindfulness involves an acceptance of experience. Mindfulness doesn't say, 'Well, I feel anxious now and that's bad.' Mindfulness just says, 'I feel anxious now.' Mindfulness is non-judgemental towards most of our experience (I will explain that 'most' in 'Non-judgemental awareness' below). So mindfulness doesn't say, 'It's raining and that's awful, especially because I am walking along the street and that's awful too.' Mindfulness says, 'Look, it's raining and I'm walking along the street.' Mindfulness doesn't bother tying itself up in a knot because it's raining. Mindfulness doesn't call you a fool for drifting away into fantasies a thousand times a day. Mindfulness just takes you back into the moment, kindly. It takes a kind interest in your foibles, your faults. Again, there is more on this below under 'Kindness'.

Mindfulness helps you break free of old patterns of thinking and reacting. It helps you to see the world and yourself in a fresh way every day. Why does this matter? Because so many of our difficulties arise from following old habits of thinking and behaving. And because the ability to take a fresh look at these habits and at our experience broadens our choices enormously. There is more on these old patterns below under 'Wakening up from the trance'.

For now, think of mindfulness as *an intentional and accepting awareness of what I experience right now*. The rest of this book is about how to cultivate that awareness and about how mindfulness benefits the human condition.

A note on history

Mindfulness as practised today was developed in the Buddhist tradition, but references to what we call mindfulness can be found in earlier Hindu texts. Buddhism made mindfulness central to its practice. In English, the word 'mindfulness' has been used since the late nineteenth century to translate the Buddhist concept of intentional and accepting awareness of present moment experience. Psychologists have been interested in mindfulness and in Buddhist psychology in general since the early twentieth century. According to Mark Epstein in *Thoughts Without a Thinker*,[1] the great American psychologist William James told a Buddhist monk, whom he spotted in the audience while giving a lecture, that 'This [Buddhism] is the psychology everybody will be studying twenty-five years from now'. James' timing was out, but as the century progressed concepts from Buddism were increasingly borrowed by the West.

In the Christian tradition, the Bombay-born Jesuit, Anthony de Mello, taught mindfulness at retreats, workshops and through books such as the classic *Awareness*.[2] His constant admonition to all who listened was to wake up to reality and get in touch with your own self through the cultivation of awareness.

Dr Jon Kabat-Zinn of the University of Massachusetts Medical School has had a major influence on the acceptance of mindfulness in the health professions through his programme, Mindfulness-Based Stress Reduction, for people suffering chronic pain and stress. Through his books – my favourite is *Wherever You Go, There You Are*[3] – Kabat-Zinn's influence has spread far outside the health sector.

Vietnamese Buddhist monk, Thich Nhat Hahn, has tirelessly promoted the practice of mindfulness from his base at Plum Village in France and through books such as *The Miracle of Mindfulness*.[4]

In the past decade, Eckhart Tolle's book, *The Power of Now*,[5] has popularised the practice of mindfulness far and wide.

Mindfulness is a practice – always

Mindfulness looks simple: just put your attention on whatever is going on for you right now. Anyone can do it! Well, yes, anyone can if they put the work into it. This appearance of simplicity is deceptive; mindfulness doesn't come naturally. Try to remain mindful – be intentionally aware of your present moment experience – for just one hour and I know you will find it impossible to do. Actually, try to do it for five minutes and you will probably find you have dipped out of mindfulness and into the imagination a hundred times.

That's why mindfulness is a practice. As simple as it may look, you must deliberately choose to practise mindfulness every day. It is a journey, not a destination. You will never reach a point at which you will be mindful without effort or intention for the rest of your life.

This impossibility of maintaining intentional awareness all the time may have something to do with the ceaseless electrical activity going on in our brains. It may also have something to do with the endless stimulation we receive through our senses. That stimulation continues even when we are asleep, otherwise the sound of a child crying or a phone ringing would have no effect.

As humans, as I will explain elsewhere, we connect one thing to another (see 'Associations and tags — when labels take over reality' in the chapter 'The Moment'). So you try to be mindful as you walk through your house, but there's that side table in the hall that you got from Aunt Ida when you moved in, and now you're back in Aunt Ida's garden as a child and there's Uncle George smoking his pipe, surrounded by that smell of tobacco you have always associated him with and then remember they had that donkey you used to ride around on ... suddenly you realise what has happened: for a few moments there you fell right out of your mindful state and into a series of linked memories. These memories are stories you tell yourself about your life. They play a role in maintaining your identity. That is why you will go back to them often, even as you practise mindfulness.

However, does the impossibility of remaining permanently mindful condemn us to failure? No, to practise mindfulness you don't have to be mindful all the time. What matters is to *return* to awareness again and again. Through returning to intentional awareness again and again we experience the benefits of mindfulness. This explains why practitioners of mindfulness are always warned to avoid reprimanding themselves for drifting away into distraction. You could reprimand all you like and still drift away. So accept that you drift away, then bring yourself back kindly to awareness each time you notice that you have wandered off. That wandering isn't failure, it's just the way things are, so accept it. And remember, when you notice you have drifted away, you have already returned to the moment.

A basic mindfulness exercise

I recommend a basic mindfulness exercise to people who attend my workshops and to counselling clients. The exercise involves connecting with what your senses bring to you. Cultivating awareness of present moment experience by connecting with your senses has been recommended as a practice for thousands of years, going back to the time of the Buddha. The body is always in the here and now, as Zen teacher Cheri Huber[6] has pointed out. Therefore, to take the royal road to mindfulness, practise awareness of what your senses bring you in the moment.

Use this basic mindfulness exercise (based on the Buddha's *Four Foundations of Mindfulness*), or your own version of it, several times a day to connect you with your here and now experience. Use it also if you feel agitated or bored or when you lie awake at night trying to sleep.

---

* Begin by noticing your breathing. You don't have to breathe in any particular way. Just notice your breathing. It might help to notice the breath entering your nostrils or your mouth and leaving again. If your mind drifts into imagination, memory or worries as you do this, just bring it back kindly to noticing your breathing.

* Now notice your posture. Are you sitting, standing, walking, lying down? Just notice.

* Notice your hands. Are your fingers bent or straight? What do your hands feel like? Are they warm or cold? Can you feel a breeze against your skin?

* What about your feet? Can you notice how they feel against your shoes or against the ground?

* Notice sounds. What are the nearest sounds you can hear? What are the furthest-away sounds you can hear?

* Notice your current emotion. Is it pleasant, unpleasant or neutral? Just notice, then back to your breathing.

* Is there a thought in your mind? Just notice, then back to your breathing.

* Now go back to noticing your breathing once more. Again, if your mind drifts into imagination, memory or worries, just bring it back kindly to noticing your breathing.

This basic exercise will take you into mindfulness whenever you do it. It doesn't matter whether you follow this sequence exactly. All that matters is connecting with your senses from time to time, those senses through which everything you know has been transmitted to you, but which we all so easily ignore in favour of the demands of the mind. Whenever I refer in this book to the basic mindfulness exercise, this is the one I mean. As you see, you can do it walking along a street, sitting at a desk or cooking a meal. Or you can close your eyes and really relax into this exercise. It is also good to do if you are awake in bed at night, but I will have more to say about this in 'How mindfulness improves your chances of a good night's sleep'.

Practice
Use this exercise first thing in the morning, a few times during the day and if you are awake in bed at night. It will bring you straight into the mindfulness zone.

Acceptance – the heart of mindfulness

Mindfulness involves the intentional awareness of your present moment experience. This is the same as saying that mindfulness involves acceptance of your experience, but what does 'acceptance' mean? It means that I face, rather than turn my back on, my experiences. In particular, instead of avoiding uncomfortable experiences, I turn towards them.

Let's say I feel tired following an interrupted night's sleep. Refusal to accept the tiredness might involve any of the following: cursing my bad luck at the interruptions that left me feeling this way; moaning on and on about how tired I am and how I wanted to be in good shape for today; taking a sleeping pill and going back to bed; and many other possibilities. In this case, a refusal to accept involves tormenting myself in many ways. The fact is, I am tired. In mindfulness, I note this and get on with things as best I can.

Let's move on to an emotion such as shame. Many people have shame inculcated in them as children – sometimes parents know no better. Because the experience of shame hurts, they may bury their awareness of it or seek to deflect other people's attention from it, for instance, through anger or boasting. But the unacknowledged shame stays and goes on influencing the person's life, eating away at their peace of mind. From time to time the shame breaks into awareness. Indeed, practising mindfulness may very well allow this buried feeling to surface.

Non-acceptance of shame may involve drinking to kill it, fighting with other people so as to replace shame with anger or hiding away. The mindfulness approach takes a different attitude. In mindfulness you note that a feeling of shame has emerged. You make no attempt to run away from it. You allow it to stay as you go about your day. You don't talk to yourself about it or re-run old scenes, but you don't try to push it away either. If your shame is an old, useless feeling from the past, noticing it in this way will allow it to fade over time, perhaps even to fade away altogether. If you feel shame over something you are doing at present, accepting the feeling allows you to make a choice. Perhaps you feel shame because you are doing the right thing; giving evidence against someone in your social circle who has committed a crime, for instance, may lead to a feeling of shame. Perhaps you feel shame because you are doing something wrong, such as exploiting another person. If I accept the shame, in other words, if I am willing to experience it without running away from it, I can then make a clear choice: give evidence or not; go on exploiting this person or not. Acceptance can lead directly to the realisation that I need to take my share of responsibility for what I do next.

Acceptance does not mean indifference to bad behaviour. A week before I began to write this book, I watched news footage of the abuse of men at a prison camp in Russia. The footage distressed me; I expect it will never entirely leave my mind. Both the torment inflicted on the men and the arrogant brutality of the guards reflected aspects of the human experience that most of us don't want to have to look at. Mindful acceptance does not mean indifference to the suffering of these men or to the behaviour of their tormentors. Mindful acceptance in this case means I accept my feelings of distress as I look at this footage. It means I am willing to experience this distress without having to get rid of the feeling. To get rid of the feeling I might have to deny what is going on, tell myself the beaten men deserve what they get or switch over to a comedy show. However, if I accept my distress then, at the very least, I can be a witness to these men's suffering, I can be more compassionate in my own behaviour or I can do something like join Human Rights Watch or Amnesty International, or perhaps write a letter to my own government asking it to object to the treatment of these prisoners.

Therefore, by accepting my distress, my shame and my tiredness, I influence my own behaviour. Acceptance leads to change and not to indifference. As authors Andrew Christensen and Neil S. Jacobson admirably put it: 'Change is the brother of acceptance, but it is the younger brother.'[7]

Practice
Notice what you are feeling right now. Can you accept that feeling without getting into a drama in your head about it?

Non-judgemental awareness

When practising mindfulness, take a non-judgemental approach to what reality brings you. By doing so you will see things freshly and make new choices. You will stand a better chance of avoiding the repetition of old habits, perhaps habits of fear or resentment, which no longer have any use. But the non-judgemental approach has its complexities too, as we'll see as we go along.

Let's look at this on a simple level first. Consider the weather. People sometimes feel under an obligation to get upset every time the rain falls, especially during the summer. Somewhere along the line they learned this formula: rain equals unhappiness. To make matters worse, if I label an experience as bad then I am more likely to see the negative sides of it than if I label it as good or neutral. If I label a windy, rainy day as 'bad' I am more likely to go around hunched up, with a look of dislike on my face than if I label it as 'interesting'. But if I label it as 'interesting' I might notice how the leaves blow in the wind, how rivulets of water run along the street and so on. So, if for a moment you take a non-judgemental approach to the rain, if you suspend your judgement on it, you may find that right now it doesn't make any great difference to you whether it's raining or not; you may even find the rain rather interesting or you may realise that you actually feel okay, even though it's raining.

Let's say you see a neighbour walking along your street who once shouted at your children when they kicked a ball into his garden and who refused to give the ball back. Every time you see this neighbour your blood pressure goes up. Perhaps you succeed in shortening your life a little every time you meet him. Your children, meanwhile, have either forgotten the whole thing or laugh at the memory. Why not suspend judgement on your neighbour next time you see him? Then at least you spare yourself the grief that goes with resenting this neighbour. You might even prolong your life at the same time!

There are other aspects, though, to this matter of being non-judgemental. Again, let's look at the simple ones first.

When I checked my email this morning, it included illustrations of two possible covers for this book. Which cover did I prefer, the publishers wanted to know? If I had emailed back to say, 'Actually, I am being non-judgemental at the moment, so I'm afraid I can't help you with this', we wouldn't get anywhere. The publishers would make a choice without my input and if I didn't like what I saw in the end, I wouldn't have a leg to stand on. What being non-judgemental in this situation means to me is to suspend judgement initially while I look at the two different covers, keeping my prejudices out of it. I try to keep away the voice that says this or that colour doesn't really go with mindfulness. I just look at the two covers with as open a mind as I can and allow a view to come to me. Then I choose – I make a judgement, but only after I have allowed myself to look at the options with an open mind.

Another example: a woman wants to buy a dress. Her choice comes down to one of two dresses. One has red stripes and the assistant thinks it suits her very well. However, the woman has a long-standing prejudice against wearing anything with red in it. If she takes a judgemental approach, then, she will say, 'Well, I never wear red or anything with red in it, so I'll have the other one'. In this instance an old judgement dictates her choice immediately. If she takes a non-judgemental approach, she can look at the two dresses, well aware of her old prejudice but opening her mind to the possibility that the dress with the red stripes suits her better than the other. Then she can make a judgement, but one based on an unprejudiced consideration of her choices.

So far I have given you fairly trivial examples, so let's move on to something more serious.

Consider the judgements made about the Jews between the First and Second World Wars, judgements of a kind that had been made about them for many centuries, especially in Europe. These judgements ultimately led to the horrors of the concentration camps and death camps. What if enough of those people, who judged the Jews harshly and unthinkingly, had taken a non-judgemental approach instead, not only in the twentieth century but in the centuries that went before? If a sufficient amount of people could have done that, perhaps those horrors could have been avoided. A non-judgemental attitude can save lives and, if taken by enough people, it can save lives by the million.

Let us suppose now that you are watching television. The camera shows a man taking the hand of a small girl and gently leading her off a beach in a Third World country. The voiceover tells you that this man, a Western tourist, has paid the girl's family to have sex with her. Where is your non-judgementalism now? Well, you can suspend judgement for a time. You can ask yourself why would this girl's parents sell her and destroy her life in this way? If it is a question of poverty then should the world, or the government of the country concerned, be doing more to alleviate the hardship of the poor? What contribution can we in the West make to this? If it's a question of law enforcement, should pressure be applied in that direction? And why is this man free to go to this country and act in this way? Should we, in our country, prosecute men who behave like this abroad? If we have laws allowing for such prosecutions, could we do more to enforce them? Should I contact my politicians or an organisation concerned with this issue to give my support? Just lifting the judgement for a few moments allows you to consider these issues, to inquire into the situation, allowing you to consider what, if anything, you might do about it. On the other hand, a purely judgemental approach might simply lead you to look at this event and say, 'That's terrible', and then go off to make yourself a nice cup of tea to help you forget about it.

A non-judgemental attitude adopted for a time – and you will probably find it's impossible to adopt it for more than a short time – can actually lead to inquiry and to action.

Now let us suppose that you are standing outside a school in your neighbourhood. A woman at the gate is handing out free samples of heroin to the children leaving the school. Is this a case for non-judgemental inquiry? Other parents are as horrified as you. Should you join them in telling this woman to leave and in calling the police? Or should you take a non-judgemental approach and inquire into the ins and outs of what brought this woman here, why a child might take the heroin and how the heroin got here? In my opinion, this is a case in which a moral imperative overcomes non-judgementalism. In the case of the paedophile you could do nothing immediately. The events depicted perhaps happened six months before they were broadcast. Suspending judgement for a short time may allow you to take some sort of action (demanding a response from politicians, for instance) against this sort of behaviour. In the case of the person distributing heroin outside the school in your presence, you can take action straight away to stop a great harm being done to children. You have arrived at the limits of the non-judgemental approach. Of course you may later, in a non-judgemental way, consider what might have driven this woman to behave in this way, but that consideration belongs to later.

To sum up, taking a non-judgemental approach does indeed give you a fresh and creative view of the people and events in your own life, and it helps you to make fresh and creative choices. Therefore, 90 per cent of the time, the non-judgemental approach is a particularly valuable element of mindfulness. Of course, we all have to make judgements in day-to-day matters, many times a day, but through suspending judgement for a time we can arrive at better, more rounded judgements in the end.

As we saw in the case of the paedophile above, suspending judgement for a time encourages you to inquire more deeply into situations and into what you might be able to do about them. However, there are some immediate situations in which a moral imperative dictates that the principle of non-judgementalism should be set aside while you act and do what needs to be done.

I should end this by acknowledging that this piece is shot through with judgements. Judgementalism is the human condition.

Practice
As you go through your day and as you find yourself disliking what you see and hear, try adopting a non-judgemental approach for a time and see what it teaches you.

Kindness

When I began to practise mindfulness I immediately found myself resisting the concept of kindness, or, rather, the practice of kindness towards myself and other people. Kindness towards myself caused me more trouble than kindness towards other people. Perhaps society taught me to devalue kindness. Or perhaps I devalued kindness as an expression of my personal psychology.

Nonetheless, I have had to work to overcome this attitude because the practice of mindfulness requires kindness towards your experience. Without kindness, mindfulness becomes another stick to beat yourself with. As I have explained elsewhere, mindfulness does not come naturally. Your mind always wanders away down byways, paths and highways and will do so again and again. Therefore, if you treat yourself harshly whenever you discover your mind has departed from the present moment, mindfulness will become more of a burden than a blessing. In that case you will only learn one lesson from mindfulness practice: that you cannot stay in the moment all the time, and you know that already. Kindness allows you to practise mindfulness for your whole life, accepting that your mind wanders around and that to berate yourself for that fact is pointless.

To better understand the value of kindness in this practice, consider what kindness contributes to one of the great benefits of mindfulness: the opening up of choices. Simply by staying in the now, by being aware of our breath or by whatever other methods we have of maintaining mindfulness (most readers will find that one or two methods from this book will become favourites), we can avoid getting stuck in a rut and going around and around the same track endlessly. Through mindfulness we have the possibility of seeing more clearly and of being able to make changes that enhance our lives.

Kindness expands choices. Harshness, by contrast, controls, it hedges in, it seeks to limit choice. Harshness kills creativity. However, kindness allows you to take a kind and open attitude to your own experiences, enables you to explore these experiences, to see what patterns of behaviour you are following and to change what you do so that you can live in a more creative way.

As with anything else, kindness taken too far can overstep moral limits – if somebody had set out to murder me, I wouldn't want the police to sit around glowing with kindness towards the would-be killer. Also, kindness comes up against a moral brick wall when it seeks to deny remorse. Remorse too can be creative; it leads people to mend their ways. To deny remorse is also to deny the possibility of change.

In general, though, I would argue that an attitude of kindness makes for a better world. In fact, human beings value kindness greatly. Many of us remember for our whole lives acts of kindness done for us by family, friends or even strangers. Children who grew up in harsh institutions remember the one person who did them an act of kindness and they hold on to that memory for their whole lives.

Think of those who act cruelly in harsh institutions, in prison camps, the workplace bullies, the school bullies, the people beating up a stranger on a street. Look at how kindness on their part could transform the world in which we live and in which they live. Look at the difference it would make.

Kindness can be radical, subversive. Those who would control us seek to confine our capacity for kindness. They know that kindness opens us up while they want to shut us down. The Provisional IRA abducted and murdered Jean McConville, a widowed mother of ten, in 1972 because of an act of kindness towards a British soldier dying on the street outside her home at Divis Flats in Belfast. The Provisionals instinctively saw how subversive an act of kindness could be towards their agenda and they quickly removed this mother in the most brutal way.

So when we advocate kindness we get into deep waters – revolutionary waters in many ways. Kindness softens a harsh world and kindness forms an essential part of the practice of mindfulness. I suggested earlier that kindness towards ourselves can, for some of us, be harder to practise than kindness towards others. If this is true of you, then persist in treating yourself kindly. Be mindful of the resistance and of the strength of that resistance. If you can stay with a practice of kindness towards yourself you may, eventually, find new paths opening that had been blocked off by your habitual harshness.

Practice
Every time you find your attention has wandered away take it back with kindness, again and again.

A kindness meditation
Here is a kindness meditation used in the Buddhist tradition. Try it and see what happens.

First, wish yourself well. You might visualise yourself or you might just talk to yourself without visualising. You could try to feel a sense of well-wishing towards yourself. Don't worry if this doesn't come the first few times you try it. Perhaps you might say to yourself silently, I wish you well. I wish you happiness.

Now think of someone you love or someone you would regard as a benefactor. This may be a person who is alive or a person who has died. Again, try to feel a sense of well-wishing towards this person. Say, I wish you well, I wish you happiness.

Now think of a person towards whom you feel neutral, perhaps the person who served you in the shop this morning. Again, try to generate that feeling of well-wishing. I wish you well, I wish you happiness.

Now think of someone you regard as irritating, a pest, annoying, a nuisance, maybe someone you think of as an enemy. Try to generate a feeling of well-wishing (it's okay, they don't know you're doing this!). I wish you well, I wish you happiness. (If you have difficulty with this, remember that if the person in question was truly well and happy they might not go around angering you or being your enemy.)

Now imagine the house or the neighbourhood or the city or the country or the planet or the universe and try to generate that feeling of well-wishing towards everybody and everything in it. I wish you well, I wish you happiness.

That's it. What are you doing with this? Changing other people? No. You are opening yourself up to a broader experience of people, of those you love, those you dislike and those you rarely think about. You are even wishing yourself well. How long is it since you did that?

Practice
Give a few minutes a day to this kindness meditation and see how it affects your feelings towards other people and towards yourself.

Euphoria warning

I began to practise mindfulness on a sunny Dublin afternoon in the 1980s. During my lunch break I had bought a book on meditation and had read two paragraphs on mindfulness. I tried it out and I liked how I felt. Later that afternoon, I abandoned my desk in *The Irish Times* – not an unusual event – and went for a stroll in the grounds of Trinity College. Cricketers were finishing a game in the late afternoon sunlight. The Pavilion Bar was open at the end of the field. I bought a beer and stood and watched the game of cricket — a game, I might add, about which I knew nothing. I felt wonderful as I practised my mindfulness. I was filled with the deepest sense of peace and happiness I had ever known. I have never forgotten the experience.

The sense of euphoria lasted for a few days. Then it went away and it has only rarely come back. This is a common experience at the start of a meditation practice. People sometimes then make the mistake of chasing that euphoria, of trying to get it back. While the feeling may come back for a few minutes or hours now and then, it is only likely to happen rarely. To be in a constant state of euphoria would, in any event, be unhelpful in many areas of your life. I wouldn't want to be operated on by a euphoric surgeon, for example! So if you experience that euphoria, enjoy it while it lasts, knowing that it will go. Adopt the attitude of the Chinese Zen master Ta-mei who, as he was dying, gave this advice to his students: 'When it comes, don't try to avoid it; when it goes, don't run after it.'[8]

Although you cannot achieve a continuous sense of euphoria through mindfulness, the many benefits of mindfulness practice are well worth the effort involved — and that effort is essentially the directing of your attention — as I hope you will find by looking through this book and practising what you find here.

Pleasant, unpleasant, neutral

We human beings tend to judge the world around us, its events and its contents, in three ways: we see experiences as pleasant, unpleasant or neutral. Our minds tend to make this judgement very quickly, so quickly we often don't notice it happening. Our tendency is to base our behaviour on those judgements.

Of course, the pleasant is what we want to experience more often. In a sense, it is what we strive to get all our lives. We tend to always move towards our pleasures and we don't feel quite ourselves when we try to cut them out or cut them down. We try to avoid the unpleasant and sometimes that avoidance becomes another major endeavour of our lives. That is unfortunate because so much — the learning of discipline, for instance – involves developing the ability to tolerate and work with experiences that are unpleasant. The neutral includes all the people and experiences that are neither pleasant nor unpleasant and that we so easily screen out of our consciousness. Indeed, the neutral probably includes most of what goes on around us. I suspect that the wider this neutral zone is for a given person, the more prone that person is to becoming bored. Again, much of what is important in life, including discipline, involves the capacity for tolerating the neutral and for many people this is a more frequent challenge than facing the unpleasant.

Curiously, the process of splitting the world into pleasant, unpleasant and neutral can take away the ability to see. With so much designated as neutral, much of life is pushed beyond awareness. Anthony de Mello SJ, in his book *Sadhana, a Way to God*,[9] talks of passengers travelling through a beautiful landscape in a train on their way to a wedding in a faraway province. The landscape through which the train travels is beautiful, but the windows of the train are covered and so the landscape may as well not exist for them. That is what consigning large areas of life into the neutral zone can do to our perceptions and experiences. Mindfulness encourages us to notice our surroundings including the things, people and events we would ordinarily classify as neutral. In this way, we bring the rest of the world back into focus and sometimes discover beauty and fulfillment we had not known was possible.

It is easier to become fixated on the pleasant than on the unpleasant or neutral aspects of experience. Do not imagine, though, that those of us who practise mindfulness take a disapproving attitude to pleasure – absolutely not, we are as fond of it as anyone else! Clearly, however, a fixation on the pleasant can also limit our experience of life. If I am so fond of my favourite TV channel that I am unwilling to abandon it for an evening, then I choose to miss out on the myriad other things that are going on. These other things could include potentially wonderful experiences. Mindfulness enables us to see this fixation in action and opens us to the possibility of making different choices. Mindfulness does something else for our pleasures too: it enables us to experience them more fully. Where is the fun in gobbling your favourite food so fast that you hardly know you are eating it? Where is the enjoyment in walking through the park and no longer noticing the trees, the grass, the flowers, the sky, the river? There is more on mindfulness and pleasure in the chapter 'Body and Mind'.

A recurrent theme of this book is the role of mindfulness in relation to the unpleasant. In mindfulness we turn towards the unpleasant and not away. This is because frantic efforts to escape the unpleasant can run us into all sorts of problems with drink, drugs, anxieties and so on. It is a driven and unsatisfactory way to live life. Encouraging us to face the unpleasant is one of the great benefits of mindfulness. You will find more on this elsewhere in the book, especially in the chapter 'Stress and Distress'.

Practice
For now, try to notice the neutral things, the things that live in the shadows of your awareness. Doing so will broaden and deepen your experience of living.

THE MOMENT

Impermanence

Almost everything you experience today will be forgotten by the time you get up tomorrow morning. This, I hope you will agree, makes a compelling argument for the practice of mindfulness. Almost all your experience belongs to the here and now – nowhere else. How many experiences did you have yesterday? Probably many thousands if you include everything that impinged on your consciousness. How many do you remember? Probably no more than two or three. A few people have photographic memories, and detailed memories of traumatic events can also, in many cases, be recalled for a long time. Most of us, though, lose our memories fairly quickly. That concert you enjoyed so much, for example, how long would it take you to run through the memories that remain of it? A few minutes?

We might look at a person with dementia and think how tragic it is. The difference may be less than you think. This phenomenon of the memory of experiences running away from us almost as soon as they have happened is one form of impermanence.

Next time you are really enjoying an event or other experience, remind yourself that almost all of this will vanish as soon as it is over and encourage yourself to maintain mindfulness so as to get the most out of it.

Another form of impermanence that is central to the practice of mindfulness is the impermanence of emotions and I refer to this many times in this book. Good emotions rise and fall and so do bad emotions or negative emotions. Mindfulness helps you to spot the good emotions when they come and helps you to enjoy them. But when they are replaced by negative emotions you know that these will also fade – no need for a big drama about it, no need to fret because good emotions pass or negative emotions come. This mindful approach, of accepting and noticing the rise and fall of emotions, can spare you a great deal of upset. However, impermanence is inherent in our very existence and in all we do. Empires, great cities, great works of art, great philosophies, you and I are all impermanent and are already changing, sometimes obviously – as a glance in the mirror tells me – and sometimes microscopically.

In the practice of mindfulness, I become aware of this impermanence and I learn to accept it, appreciating ordinary experiences in a way that simply would not happen if I knew that everything around me on this earth was going to last forever.

Practice
Let the awareness of impermanence deepen your practice of mindfulness and this in turn will deepen your experience of life as it happens.

What quality am I bringing to this moment?
This question, if you ask it, can bring you straight into the practice of mindfulness – so long as you don't answer it.

I find that asking this question lights up my awareness of whatever is going on right now and it reminds me that my experience is coloured by what I bring to events as well as by events themselves. Rain is external; the quality I bring to being in the rain is mine; together they make up my experience.

Why not answer the question? Because the purpose of the question is to put me in touch with my experience. As soon as I try to answer it, I spin off into a useless sequence of thoughts and intellectualising. The intellectual mind might assert that there is no such thing as a moment – you can't take a moment and analyse it, put it in a jar and stick a label on it. That's not a problem; I don't mind whether there is or is not such a thing as a moment. When I say 'this moment' I'm really saying 'the experience that I am having right now'. And so, when I ask what quality I bring to this moment, I'm really asking what quality I bring to this experience, what is my relationship to this experience? What is the meaning of 'quality', the mind asks? No, this is not Philosophy 101. Just ask the question: what quality am I bringing to this moment? That is all you have to do.

Another reason for not answering the question is that if you do, you may end up criticising yourself for not bringing the 'right' quality to the experience. But you are not asking the question to judge your level of perfection! You are asking it in order to get in touch with whatever is going on. I find that as soon as I ask the question, I get an immediate sense of detachment from whatever is going on in my head. I don't mean detachment in the sense of uninvolvement or of not appreciating what is going on; I mean detachment in the sense that I become aware of myself in this experience. I get a sense of spaciousness. I am no longer caught up in my own mind. I could be bringing anything to the experience: mindfulness, anger, tiredness, wanting or joy, to mention a handful of possibilities. However, I find that the answer is simply irrelevant. The purpose of asking the question is to get me back into an aware relationship with whatever is going on. Once I have asked the question, I am brought into that relationship and I don't need an answer.

Practice
As you go through your day, stop frequently and ask yourself: 'What quality am I bringing to this moment?' Don't answer. Simply asking the question puts you in touch with your experience.

What is this? Returning again and again to mindfulness
Here is another question to return you quickly to a sense of mindfulness throughout your day: *what is this?*

As with other questions that help in our practice of mindfulness, the answer really doesn't matter. Moreover, you don't want to spin off into an intellectual analysis: you just want to get in touch with experience. Asking the question is enough to do this and to deepen your practice of mindfulness.

As you ask, you may feel surprised at how many details of your life go on in the background, just outside your awareness. For instance, I am sitting in my office and I ask myself, *what is this?* I become aware of light and shadow, the green plant on the mantelpiece, the way the sunlight falls on the bricks of a building across the way. As I walk along a street I ask, *what is this?* and I notice the ornate upper floors of buildings that I have passed many times but never pay attention to. Perhaps I notice the sound of a solitary bird competing with the traffic. Similarly, when I am out walking or running, asking the question brings my attention to the sky, to trees, to the river and perhaps to the hundreds of birds that are singing in my surroundings, but that are usually outside my awareness.

It is as though early in life we look through a clear window at the world. Gradually, we get so caught up in our own thoughts, emotions and experiences that we replace the window with a mirror. We no longer see objective reality; instead we see a picture made up of all the things that have been 'experienced' by the mirror. So eventually, instead of looking through that clear window, we look into a distorting mirror, like a carnival mirror – though the reflection isn't necessarily always funny!

Some meditators ask *what is this?* in order to gain new insights into their experience. However, when I'm practising mindfulness that's not why I'm asking the question. I'm asking the question because it brings me straight into a mindful state from which I will inevitably have drifted. It replaces that distorting mirror with a clear, clean window, if only for a moment.

I am not doing this simply in order to become aware of details. I am doing it in order to experience the long-term benefits of mindfulness: relaxation, appreciation and a general enhancement of the quality of my life. Sometimes, if I am lucky, I notice some useful truths about my own self or my behaviour. Perhaps I am busy being annoyed, for instance, because the world is inexplicably refusing to revolve around me. Noticing this gives me the opportunity to ask if this is a useful way to conduct myself.

Note that what you see with mindfulness will not always be comforting. Here is another analogy: you are driving along in heavy rain in the dark. The windscreen and windows are fogged up by your

own breath. You could be in a panic be/
glimpses of darkness, rain and shadow.
you are on a perfectly safe road. Or you c.
on a perfectly safe road and be, in reality, abou.
By asking *what is this?* we seek to clean the windscre.
is going on. Mindfulness is not always comforting, bu.
improves your chances of seeing clearly what is necessary — an.
is worth having.

Practice

To broaden your awareness and your experience of mindfulness,
remember to ask yourself what is this? *when you are out walking*
or at your desk or, indeed, on any occasion.

What am I doing here? Mindfulness of intention

We are always paying attention to something: an email, a fantasy, the
food on our plate, a memory. But attention left to itself, so to speak,
is hijacked continually by the next thing that comes along.
Mindfulness is attention with intention. In mindfulness, we
deliberately pay attention to our experience. You could say that
deliberate attention is mindfulness.

Awareness of intention can be a useful mindfulness practice in
itself. In this practice, you continually return to an awareness of your
wider intention in what you are doing. Right now, as I write this,
my intention is to produce a few hundred words on this particular
mindfulness exercise. I am not floating around in some sort of
dream; I have an intention and I know what it is. I would like to have
a cup of tea so I go out to the kitchen, wait for the kettle to boil, find
myself wandering around the living room and remind myself that my
intention is to make a cup of tea, bring it back to my desk and get
on with the writing. Later on I will have other intentions: meeting
someone, making dinner, driving safely from Point A to Point B and
so on.

In all of this, old habit patterns can sweep me away at any time. Let
us say I meet somebody whom I haven't seen for a while. I want the

...ing to go well, but then there they go with that irritating habit of ...icising something the moment they open their mouth. Suddenly I ...m brought into old reaction patterns. I am no longer as warm or as welcoming as I had wanted to be. We could very easily have a row if I respond as I have always responded, but if I can be mindful of my intention to have an encounter that is warm and enjoyable for us all, then I can spot that old reaction starting up and I can deflect it by recalling my intention to have a different encounter this time.

If I go into a meeting at work with the intention of remaining calm and logical in the face of provocation, I can quite easily get swept away by the aggression and negativity of certain other people. But if I retain my mindfulness of intention, when others become aggressive or negative I can simply and calmly continue to promote my point of view. This is an especially useful approach in dealing with unpleasant people at work – maintaining your presence of mind is half the battle.

Perhaps my intention is to go upstairs, make the bed and put away the clothes I left lying on the floor last night. How often have I gone up the stairs and come back down without having done what I went up there for in the first place? By maintaining awareness of my intention in going upstairs I have a better chance of getting the bed made and the clothes off the floor.

Awareness of intention can provide a sort of thread to guide you through the day in an effective way. Needless to say, you will get lost now and then, but you can keep coming back to the thread of intention.

Practice
Asking what is my intention? *or* what am I doing here? *is an excellent way to cultivate mindfulness – and it can make you more effective in your day.*

Wakening up from the trance
We often think of a trance as a state induced by a hypnotist. The subject sits still, eyes closed, and obeys the instructions of the hypnotist. You would not want to cook a meal, do a day's work or drive down a motorway in a hypnotic trance.

In fact, we live in a sort of trance much of the time without realising it. We even cook meals, work and drive along motorways in a trance. This is not a good way to be. Mindfulness breaks the trance by helping us to notice it and thereby freshens up our view of life. I do not mean to say that we are all going through our days in the sort of deep trance a skilled hypnotist might put us into. Rather, think of our condition as living in a light trance, one that lets us get through our tasks more or less safely but which, if we don't realise what's going on, can rule our life.

Let me explain the process. (I have borrowed this explanation from Buddhist psychology.) The trance happens in stages.

First, something happens. That something could be an event in the external world – a phone ringing, for example – or it could be something that happens internally – a sudden little spike in anxiety, let us say. We react to these events instantly. We may react with a sense of gladness. For example, if you have been waiting for that phone call from somebody you very much want to talk to, you will be glad to hear the phone ring. We can also react with a sense of aversion: I may shy away from that spike of anxiety. Or, indeed, one might simply react with a 'so what?' Perhaps we might even be so indifferent that we never get as far as 'so what?' As I sit here writing this, cars pass by my window, but I fail to notice them most of the time.

This reaction of what I'm going to call gladness or rejection or 'so what-ness' happens so fast that we don't usually notice it occurring, but the gladness and the rejection bring with them a whole raft of associations. Perhaps I have been waiting for that phone call from someone whom I would very much like to see, someone I have fallen in love with even. So when the phone rings and I see her number coming up on the screen, the associations begin to flood in. In my mind's eye I see her image, perhaps I remember the last time I was with her, I construct a fantasy of the meal I'm planning to take her for tonight. This whole array of pictures, memories and fantasies leaps to life in my mind in a flash. In a sense, I'm suddenly relating to these and not to the actual person who is ringing my phone. In a sense, I have gone into a light trance.

Similarly, with the spike of anxiety, my mind may instantly search for a reason to be anxious. That anxiety may have arisen from some little hormonal blip in my body, some small event that really has little meaning in the great scheme of things. But I need to attribute my anxiety to something and so I might think of a meeting I have tomorrow morning at work that I am not looking forward to at all. Suddenly I am visualising the people at the meeting, the issues, the importance of putting up a good show, the consequences of failing to impress and so on. Again, I am in a light trance.

Back to the new love of my life. I answer the phone with a mind full of pleasant pictures of the last time I saw her and of the evening I have planned for both of us. But maybe she wants to spend some time alone tonight. Maybe she needs a little space. My disappointment when I hear this is great. After all, this picture – of her alone in her place and me alone in my place – never entered my head. I had been too busy with my trance. Now I'm upset. I may even think her unreasonable. I may have a row with her over it.

So when I am in the grip of these associations I am really no longer contacting the fresh, here and now reality of the moment. But the process goes further than that. What I am now in danger of doing is creating a new reality that conforms to my trance.

Let's say I worry so much about that meeting at work that I cannot sleep properly the night before. I go into the meeting worn out and ill-prepared. I feel I do badly. In a sense, I have brought about an unpleasant reality thanks to my trance. Perhaps the others at the meeting were satisfied with my presentation, but I get so caught up in my negative trance that I fail to notice this. And what about the row with my new love? Suppose she doesn't talk to me for the rest of the week because I started a row over her desire to spend some time on her own? Has my trance not created that reality too?

You could object, reasonably, that things could have worked out differently. She might be delighted to go out to dinner with me tonight. I might prepare so well for the meeting that I sleep like a baby and put on a great show the next day. And if everything always worked out beautifully for us, we would all stay in our trances! That, as we know, is not how life works out.

It is better to have choices based on a clear view of what reality brings us. In other words, we need to take back control of our choices from the trance-like state into which it is so easy to slip. We need to get a life, to get into contact with the freshness of the world in which we live for such a short time.

Practice
Notice the associations that spring to life as you go through your day. Then get into contact with what your present moment reality is bringing you.

Habit energy – how routine can make life stale
My favourite stretch of the River Liffey runs along by the beautiful Memorial Park in Dublin, maintained in memory of Irish people who died in two world wars. I like to walk through the park and then along the river to Chapelizod, the setting for James Joyce's *Finnegans Wake*.

When I first began to walk there I was enthralled by the effect of light on the trees, the singing of birds and the general loveliness of that stretch of river. It was like walking into another world, even another life. How, I wondered, could I ever fail to be alive to this? Yet, as time went on I found I could walk along the river entirely absorbed in my own thoughts and oblivious of the beauty around me.

'Habit energy', as the Buddhists call it, had come into play. Habit energy is routine, it is getting used to performing certain actions so you don't have to think about them, even getting used to people and places so they don't claim all your attention. Habit energy is useful: it can help you to drive a car, ride a bicycle and do other such things without having to think out every move every time. But it can also mean that you lose the freshness of your experience of people and places. So while habit energy helps you with routines, it can also put blinkers on you and thereby keep you plodding along the same old tracks, your mind a hundred miles away. The practice of mindfulness is a great antidote to the lulling effect of habit energy.

If this was all that mindfulness achieved it would be enough. Mindfulness keeps the wonder alive. It keeps your eyes open. However, habit energy affects relationships. You may be in the habit, for example, of criticising and blaming your partner every day. At worst, this behaviour can destroy your marriage. At best, it can take the good out of it. Indeed, two people can shout at each other for years without once realising that all this shouting is useless and that they need to find another way to negotiate their relationship. Habit energy blinds them to the pointlessness of their behaviour. In effect, they have given their relationship over to that habit energy, to the urge to go on repeating old behaviours.

Among the most important relationships you will ever have is the relationship with yourself. Habit energy shapes this relationship too. You may be in the habit of seeing yourself in a negative or positive way and from time to time, no doubt, you behave in ways that merit one or other of these points of view. But to see yourself in the same way all the time can be dangerous. For instance, if you are in the habit of seeing yourself as helpless, you may deny yourself many experiences that you are perfectly capable of having and instead you may find yourself falling into depression or into manipulative behaviours.

By helping us to spot habitual behaviours – to spot habit energy at work in ourselves – mindfulness enables us to see new ways of doing things, it enables us to make fresh choices. This is not to say that we must drop all our habits or make fresh choices every second of the day – that would make for a rather tiring, if interesting, life! But mindfulness helps us to discriminate between useful habits and those that impoverish or harm our lives, especially in our relationships with other people and with ourselves.

The general practice of mindfulness enriches our experience in large measure by making us aware of the power of habit energy in our lives. This book has many direct techniques for working with habit energy and you will find some of them in the following sections: 'What quality am I bringing to this moment?'; *'What is this?* Returning again and again to mindfulness'; and 'Cues – calling back the wandering mind'.

Associations and tags – when labels take over reality

The brain helps us to 'know' the world by attaching associations or what we might call 'tags' to our experiences and to our perceptions. At a basic level, the concept of a bird is tagged with other concepts such as 'feathers', 'beak', 'nest', 'eggs' and so on. You can see how this tagging helps us to make sense of the world, to classify objects for instance.

But we also attach emotional tags, which interfere with our perception of present-day reality. When I see my computer, I experience a mental state of interest and curiosity, because I know that through it lies access to the whole world of the internet and because the arrival of computers transformed my way of working and much of my way of living outside work.

Mindfulness helps us to notice these tags. It gives us a mental space in which to assess whether they are helpful or not: would I benefit from less time at a screen and more time out and about, for instance?

Tagging has its uses, though, as I noted above. Attaching a 'danger' and 'murder' tag to dark alleys helps us to stay out of these places at night, which is good, even though most dark alleys do not contain murderers. But emotional tags stretching way back into the past can swamp our present experience.

Suppose I see a colleague walk into work. She criticised me at a staff meeting last year about one of my pet projects, so I have tagged her 'critic' and maybe 'enemy'. Perhaps she shares that tag with a stern former teacher of mine who has tags such as 'cruel' or 'unfair'. So all the emotions that go with these tags are stirred when my colleague walks in the door. Together they make up a lot of emotions extending back over many years. They can sweep me away and make me resentful, even though my colleague may have nothing but goodwill towards me and may be completely unaware of how she offended me.

In a sense, then, tags create my experience. Suppose walking in the park is tagged in my mind with attractive associations: a sense of freedom, pleasant foliage, a feeling of well-being. I will look for these things when I am next in the park. I will look for the leaves, the flowers, the birdsong, the feeling of healthy exercise and so on. But if my tags are of boredom, time wasted, uneven ground, then I am far more likely on my next walk to feel bored, to notice the unevenness of the ground, to see that ugly shed of corrugated iron in the middle of a field and so on. So the tags have created my experience of walking in the park.

Mindfulness helps us to spot the tags and to make new choices. When you practise mindfulness and you meet that colleague whom you resent, those feelings are still likely to arise. However, there is now a good chance that you will notice the whole symphony starting up, with all its resentments and memories of past injustices carried out not just by her, but by people she has never even met. Simply by spotting this you can be open to the possibility that she may behave differently this time. Perhaps her criticism at that meeting was not meant as an attack, but was interpreted by you in that way. On the other hand, perhaps it really was an attack. Either way, though, mindfulness allows you to see your old reactions surfacing and to deal with each day and each encounter in a fresh way.

Sometimes the tags work in our favour, especially when seen clearly in mindfulness. Here is that dark alley. It's midnight. Your street is at the other end. Cutting through the dark alley will get you home three minutes sooner than if you walk around it. Mindfulness of the fact that you have put a 'danger' tag on dark alleys and for a good reason may help you to decide to go the long way around and, as a result, may save your life.

Mindfulness of the associations we attach to experiences also helps in dealing with addictions or with strongly habitual behaviours. A person who is trying to stay off cocaine, for instance, may find that when they go to a certain part of the city and meet certain friends in certain places the temptation to use cocaine again becomes very, very strong. That is because this place and these friends are tagged with all the associations that go with using cocaine, including craving. Mindfulness of what is going on increases the chances of avoiding relapse and may underline the importance of staying away from certain places and people.

These tags are not just like passive labels tied to your luggage. They carry an èmotional charge and they influence your behaviour. Indeed, you could think of tags and associations as similar to the Buddhist idea of karma: your previous actions have sown certain seeds, which come to life when you encounter certain reminders, and they help push you towards repeating the experience. This is somewhat similar to the old Catholic idea of an occasion of sin. The idea here is that if you enter a situation in which you are influenced towards doing wrong, then you are more likely to do wrong again.

Tags are useful because they represent an accumulation of experience and they help us to navigate our way through the world. However, because they can take control of our perceptions and reactions, we need to know that they exist and that they are at work in us. Mindfulness helps to bring us that awareness and helps us to make freer choices about what to do next. Mindfulness makes a space in which new responses to old situations can arise. Mindfulness, therefore, is creative. In a world full of tags and associations, it enables us to see more clearly and to experience life differently.

Practice
Now and then when walking down a street or meeting someone, ask yourself what mental tags you might have added to this place or person in the past and consider whether there isn't a great deal more to them than this.

HUSTLE AND BUSTLE

Cues – calling back the wandering mind

As I point out constantly in this book, practising mindfulness means more than deciding that from now on I will be aware of my present moment experience as it occurs. In the busyness of our lives, the mind distracts itself too easily for that, behaving like a flock of sheep on a country road. If you have ever herded sheep along a road you will know that every gap in a hedge, every open gate, every lane attracts them – and off they go. That is why God invented sheepdogs: to turn the sheep back onto the road they were supposed to be on and to do this as many times as necessary.

Mindfulness cues work just like sheepdogs. They herd the wandering mind back to the moment time and again. To work with cues, especially in the rather rushed times in which we live, you need to pick a couple of routine activities, activities so routine you usually do them with your mind a million miles away, then decide that in future you will do them in awareness. In effect, these routine actions will call you back to mindfulness again and again, just like sheepdogs on the country road.

Examples of such actions might be: in the home: showering, cleaning, going up and down the stairs, washing up, walking through the hallway; at work: reaching for the phone, logging on to your computer, using the lift, clocking in; elsewhere: driving (what does the steering wheel feel like?), walking along your street, looking around you in a café.

You might use the path, perhaps between your front door and your front gate (or the corridor between the door of your apartment and the lift or stairs) to recall you to mindfulness many times a day. Is there a particular point you pass every day when you leave work, a landmark or a shop for instance? Why not see that as a mindfulness cue to get you out of revolving work issues in your head and into awareness of the moment?

My mindfulness cues include splashing water on my face in the mornings to wake myself up and grinding coffee for my first caffeine rush of the day. Mindfulness cues that kick in when you get up in the morning help give you a distance from gloomy or anxious morning thoughts. Sometimes, if I'm facing what looks like a tough day, these moments of mindfulness give me time and space to simply suspend judgement on the day, and choosing to suspend judgement gives me a better start than telling myself it's going to be a lousy day. Non-judgemental awareness is, I might add, a key component of mindfulness (see 'Non-judgemental awareness' in the 'Introductions and Explanations' chapter), therefore, suspending judgement on the day is entirely in line with this approach. By the way, if you are one of those lucky people who spring up in the morning full of the joys of living, never mind the 'suspending judgement' part – enjoy the joy for as long as it lasts!

Practice
To bring yourself back to mindfulness again and again, pick some routine actions from your day and decide to use one or two of them to remind you to be mindful.

The Lake – a practice in broad awareness

Sit in one place for ten to twenty minutes. Try to be aware of whatever happens around you without wandering off in your imagination. Of course, you will inevitably wander off but as soon as you spot this happening, quickly notice where your mind has brought you and then take yourself back to the scene around you. Are there other people around? Notice their posture, what emotions they seem to be experiencing – just notice. Notice your breathing as you observe.

I call this practice 'The Lake' because a lake undergoes many experiences over the centuries or millennia, but always returns to calm. It may experience storms, drought, boats, jet skis, swimmers, fishers, fish, birds, plants, things being dumped into it and a million and one other things. Still, the lake absorbs them and returns to calm.

Sometimes I do this practice having a coffee in the city, giving my awareness to the sights and sounds of the city and to the taste of the coffee. At other times I do the practice sitting in my car at the end of a run or walk. Usually, my mind has a field day, going off in all directions, getting caught up in its own contents. There I am sitting in the Phoenix Park, practising awareness of trees, clouds, blue or grey sky, the wheels of other cars on gravel, grass moving in the wind, the voices of walkers or runners, dogs barking, birdsong and many other things. I notice a herd of deer grazing in the distance. Suddenly I am in Mr Thomas's Chop House in Manchester eating the first and only venison I have ever had. Next, if I am not careful, I will be in the Royal Exchange Theatre at that farce we saw the following night, full of vicars scarpering around the stage. But I realise what is happening and I pull my mind out and return to awareness of what is actually going on in the present.

Spotting myself going off on these excursions and bringing myself gently back each time somehow helps me to feel 'freer' for the rest of my day, more able to get a sense of detachment from events that might otherwise push me along. As importantly, maybe even more so, I am more able to enjoy experiences that I might otherwise drift away from: conversations, a meal, an interesting piece of work, a walk along the canal, a piece of music. Broad awareness is enjoyable, relaxing and liberating. It is doing nothing for twenty minutes but knowing you are doing nothing. It's not as easy as you think – try it and see!

Practice
Try broad awareness while sitting at your desk, when walking, in a café, in the garden or park. Allow your attention to embrace many experiences and not just those that habitually grab it.

Patience – a side-effect of mindfulness

Is our society more impatient than societies of the past? I'm not sure that it is, despite appearances. Impatient societies have always existed, especially in cities. The Roman philosopher Seneca railed against busyness and impatience in the time of Nero. In our own time, though, I suspect most of us probably live in what might be called an impatient setting.

Actually, we as human beings have managed to turn impatience almost into an art form. Technology allows for so much to happen without delay and I must admit I quite like the immediacy that is central to our lives today. I'm not asking to retreat to an island and sit there patiently waiting for nothing in particular to happen, though no doubt to do so would be good for my soul! Nonetheless, a little extra patience can give us a valuable mental space: time to 'be' and not only time to 'do'. Running to keep up with technology can be exhausting and a little patience helps us to slow down to a human pace.

The practice of mindfulness tends to cultivate patience. Impatience is very often driven by a rush of thoughts; in mindfulness we learn to observe our thoughts, let them float on by and not be pushed around by them. In that way, mindfulness cultivates patience. In mindfulness also we notice so much more of the 'ordinary' world: the sky, the style of a car, a raindrop on a leaf, everyday sounds in the house, light and shade. In mindfulness we pause, we give these things our attention and, as a consequence, we naturally arrive at a more patient way of living. Indeed, if you find yourself hurrying in an unhelpful way to complete a task, try switching into a mindfulness mode and you will find that the little extra patience this gives you will help you do a better job. I would not for a second advocate unending patience though – such frustration! We need enthusiasm and excitement too.

Practice
From time to time, deliberately act patiently in mindfulness. See how this changes the tone of your experience.

Bully at work

Ellen says: 'I arrive at work fearing the worst. Day in, day out a colleague makes hurtful remarks. I have long learned there is nothing I can do to appease her. Any response I make draws more sarcasm.'

Many people are in Ellen's position and know too well the pain of bullying in the workplace. What can mindfulness do for Ellen and for other people in her situation? Mindfulness can give Ellen a mental space in which to choose how to respond to her tormentor. It can give her a presence of mind that bullying in the workplace all too easily sweeps away. Faced with an unpleasant work colleague or a bully, most of us fall into automatic reactions. These reactions are understandable but not always helpful. For example, it is common for the target of bullying to try to appease the bully, to twist and turn to stop the bullying – especially if the bully is a boss.

However, if what is going on is bullying, rather than tough management, the appeasing and twisting and turning won't work. This is because the bully may be acting out of irrational motives, may enjoy bullying other people or may want to push somebody out of their job in favour of a friend or relative.

When appeasement or a request for the bullying to stop fails, the target may obsess mentally about it, go over and over bullying incidents in the mind, lie awake all night, skip eating properly and so on. In a sense, the bully has taken control of the target's own mind. The target goes on suffering even while the bully plays golf or sleeps. It is as though the target feels under an obligation to go on tormenting himself or herself, as if this damaging and pointless response can somehow help to resolve matters. Mindfulness can break this cycle of destructive reactions. In mindfulness you understand that you cannot control the bully, but you can take back control of your own mind, your own behaviours. By detaching from your obsession with the bullying, you gain distance from it and start to regain peace of mind. The obsessing will seek to return, but whenever it does you simply return to mindfulness of breathing, of sounds, of posture (the basic mindfulness exercise earlier in this book will help you to do this). In this way you avoid replaying bullying scenes or thoughts about the bullying again and again. Let's say you learn to pay attention to your breathing while your bully is banging on at you. See how you have taken control of your side of the interaction? You cannot control the bully but you can control what you do.

Mindfulness involves acceptance, so you accept you are being bullied. What next? Ask the bully to stop? This may work if the bully doesn't realise what he or she is doing. If this doesn't work then you accept this fact and you talk, perhaps to the union or your boss. And if this doesn't work you may have to accept this as well and move to another department or get a new job (but ideally don't leave until the new job is in the bag). Mindfulness gives you a space in which to make these and other choices. What you are doing all the time with all this mindfulness and acceptance is taking care of your own side of the encounter and letting the bully take care of his or hers. If the bully says something nasty and you cringe like a beaten dog, you will feel very bad afterwards. If you flare up and lose control, you may get yourself into a lot of trouble (bullies can be quick to make a bullying complaint against the very person they themselves have been tormenting all along). So mindfulness during your encounters with the bully is a key response to cultivate. When your bully makes a nasty criticism you might say: 'What exactly is it that you want me to do differently?' or, 'I disagree with your point of view but if that is your point of view, so be it' or, 'If you continue to speak to me in this way, I will take the matter further.'

The response depends on the situation. Some of the above may be right for your situation, but perhaps none of them are. What matters, as I said above, is that you take charge of your response; you do not expect to control the behaviour of the bully because that is essentially outside your control. You may try to influence the bully but you do not try to control them, otherwise you simply end up criticising yourself when it doesn't work. What you seek to do through mindfulness is control your own actions and reactions in the face of the bully. This will help you to feel a great deal better than allowing the bully to dictate the whole scenario, even down to your own thinking. It may even make the bully back off, though this is not guaranteed. The key thing is that you come out of the experience in better psychological shape than if you react in an automatic way. This is all easier said than done in the heat of the moment, though, isn't it? Yet cultivating mindfulness can help to take the heat out of the moment and enable you to make choices about your responses as the encounter takes place. It enables you to see that while your mind may want you to cringe, fly into a temper or run away, you have another choice: to respond assertively out of your own dignity as a human being.

Of course, you do not cultivate mindfulness in the middle of the encounter with your bully, you cultivate mindfulness in daily life. In this way you prepare yourself to be assertive in the encounter, but you also gain the other benefits of mindfulness, especially the benefits which arise from not obsessing about your situation. Bullying is an unpleasant and sometimes shattering aspect of life, especially in the present day, but mindfulness can help you to get through it with a minimum of damage to yourself.

Practice
If you are being bullied in the workplace, watch out for obsessive thinking. Instead, use mindfulness as a tool to help you get through this experience in good shape.

How mindfulness makes for better planning

Can you plan for the future while practising mindfulness? Absolutely! Because mindfulness involves maintaining, as best you can, awareness of your current experience you may wonder how it can be compatible with future planning. Not only does mindfulness not clash with planning, it leads to even better planning on the part of those who practise it.

The fact is that much of what passes for planning has little connection with real planning. Let's suppose you remember you need to get some quotes for car insurance by the end of the month. Perhaps you immediately have a vision in your mind of waiting for ages and ages on some awful automated telephone system that you remember from the last time you called. Next your mind shows you a re-run of that time you dented the wing of the car by backing into a tree when you were trying to find your dog in a dark lane at night. The voiceover asks: 'Remember how long it took to get the claim sorted out and the repairs done?' 'How did that dog get out anyway?'

What has happened here is that you set out to plan to get the best price you can for your car insurance, but now you have wandered off into a morass of memories. Can you call that planning? I think not.

When you take a mindful approach you allow the memories to pass on by. You look up the telephone numbers of two or three insurance companies to ring for a quote. That is planning. Mindful planning works better than upsetting yourself with memories and fantasies. You don't plan in memory or in fantasy, you plan in the here and now. Mindful planning is particularly helpful when you face tasks that you don't want to do but have to do anyway.

For instance, take that phone call you really don't want to make to that person you really don't want to talk to. What would be helpful, as a plan, would be to write down the telephone number and a few points you want to make. Without a mindful approach, though, you might fall into a fantasy about the conversation that will take place, perhaps recycling resentments towards the person before you ring them and so on. Next thing you know, the phone rings, you hear the voice of the ogre at the other end and you are caught off guard. Better a little mindful planning!

Consider the value of mindfulness in relation to the to-do lists with which we torment ourselves. Have you ever noticed that your lists contain many fairly simple items that you never seem to reach? Actually, the items on a to-do list can connect with all sorts of fears and memories, often at a subconscious level. Perhaps a teacher shamed you in front of your classmates because you made a mess of writing a letter as homework. Now a to-do item such as 'Write to AB re. XY' mysteriously never gets done because your mind, affected by that old memory, shies away from the task.

A mindful approach might involve looking at your to-do list, prioritising it in some sensible way and noticing the emotions that tug at you as you consider the list. Realising that the origins of these emotions may very well be unconscious, accepting that the emotions are there and then planning to get on with doing the things that matter most all form part of mindful planning – far less complicated than the dramas which go on in our heads in the name of planning but which are not really planning at all. Indeed, you could even make working on your to-do list an exercise in mindfulness itself. Do that and see what happens. I think you will be pleased with the results.

Finally, a word of warning: put to-do lists into perspective. I once saw a cartoon showing a headstone in a graveyard bearing the following motto: 'Got everything done, died anyway.'

Practice
Plan mindfully, watching out for the unhelpful tendency of the mind to wander off into memories and fantasies.

BODY AND MIND

Breathing – a foundation of mindfulness practice

Awareness of breathing has been a foundation of mindfulness for more than two thousand years. Breathing is always available while you are alive. It's free; you don't have to stump up money to a multi-national corporation for the latest in breathing. To be aware of your breathing is to be aware of your present moment experience. Therefore, breathing on its own is a complete mindfulness practice, so long as you are paying attention to it.

Here is an interesting thing about your breath: your parents breathed, so did their parents and their parents and their parents and so on all the way back to the first humans in Africa. From the time the first human drew breath, right down to you, there has been a thread of breathing, of breath, of inhalation and exhalation, and this will go on for as long as there are human beings. If you like, we are part of one great breath that encompasses the whole existence of our species.

For you, your breath is part of your history. It is not a mechanical thing, the same in everyone at all times. From your parents you may have learned to breathe in certain ways, perhaps deeply, perhaps shallowly; perhaps you have learned to exhale fully, perhaps only partially. It is the same with inhaling: perhaps you restrict it. As the Gestalt therapists point out, restricting your breathing can be a way to avoid feelings of excitement, and your personal history or your culture may have seen such excitement as dangerous or, at least, to be approached with caution. On the other hand, the people who influenced you may have valued excitement and you may reflect this in your breathing.

So mindfulness of breathing is not a simple or boring thing. It is a mindfulness connected with your whole history, back to the origins of humanity and also to your own emotional history and to the way you regulate your feelings. So let's look at some ways in which you can be mindful of breathing. Try these and see which work best for you.

CHECKING IN WITH THE BREATH: Checking in with your breathing provides a quick and useful way to get in touch with your present moment experience. The method couldn't be simpler. As you go through your day, notice your breathing from time to time. All you need to do is notice: you don't have to breathe in any special way. You could notice one or more of the following: is your breathing different now to what it was a few minutes ago? Is it calmer or more laboured? Are you breathing with your chest or your tummy (abdominal breathing is usually more relaxing)? As you breathe, can you feel movement in your diaphragm (between your chest and your abdomen)? Can you feel the air entering and leaving your nostrils?

No need to learn that list off by heart, by the way, and no need to run through all the questions every time. I've included them only to give you an idea as to how to check in. Just to feel the air entering and leaving through your nostrils is enough.

In this practice also, you are not being asked to breathe in a particular way. Mindfulness doesn't prescribe how to do what you do; it is about noticing what you are doing while you are doing it and noticing what your senses are bringing to you.

ONE BREATH IN, ONE BREATH OUT: Every now and then pause. Breathe in and out in awareness. You may be sitting at your desk, working in the kitchen, stalled in traffic – all these situations and many others provide an opportunity to do this simple exercise.

NOTICE GAPS IN BREATHING: Sometimes you can stop breathing without even noticing that you are doing so. As you increase your awareness of breathing, you will notice this from time to time. You may find you pause breathing as you ponder something, as you do something you don't want to do (the equivalent of holding your nose in disgust, I suppose) or at other times that have some link with your own emotional history. Stopping your breathing may be a way to block excitement and engagement. See if spotting this happening makes a difference.

10 PER CENT: Can you give 10 per cent of your attention to your breathing as you carry out tasks or walk, read or watch TV? Of course, at times you need to give 100 per cent of your attention to what you are doing, but when you can give that 10 per cent, it will anchor you to the moment. It will also give you a sense of autonomy in the moment.

FORMAL BREATH PRACTICE: Sit still. Notice that you are breathing in and out. Notice the in-breath and the out-breath. If you are breathing through your nose, notice the air is colder when entering your nose than when leaving. When thoughts come into your mind just let them float on by. Do not get involved with them. If you like you can just label your thoughts: when you get a thought, just say to yourself, 'Thought', then simply go back to noticing your in-breaths and out-breaths. You may find that paying attention to your out-breath for a time is especially calming. If you like, you can count your breaths, counting from one to ten and then back to one again. If you feel uncomfortable in your body, simply take your awareness back to your breathing. If you feel pain, simply take your awareness back to your breathing. Do this for five to twenty minutes, once or twice a day.

Practice

Make awareness of your breathing a constant part of your mindfulness practice. 'One breath in, one breath out' is an excellent way to do this.

Body scan

We live in an odd age in which, in the West at any rate, the use of images of the body to sell goods and services has reached a height it has never reached before. Pornography and erotica proliferate to an unheard of extent.

Yet in this apparently sensuous world, this world of images, many, many people have little awareness of their bodies except when their bodies hurt them. It is as though we live in our minds and push away the full sense of our own bodily feelings. Yet experience is sensual. Everything we know comes to us through our senses. Even our thoughts are generated by physical brain cells through a flow of physical electricity and physical chemicals. What we see, hear, smell and taste all comes through the physical senses. The body scan is a mindfulness exercise that aims to get us back in touch with that physical reality.

To do a body scan, lie down or sit comfortably and just feel a wave of awareness moving from your toes, through your legs, along your trunk, up your back, through your arms, through your shoulders, up your neck into your head and face and then feel that awareness moving down again. You can do this relatively quickly or you can do it very slowly.

If you are not working with a counsellor or with a mindfulness group or meditation teacher, I do not suggest you do lengthy (for example, forty-five-minute) sessions because the body scan can bring up memories of experiences long suppressed. This can be difficult and frightening to deal with on your own.

However, body scans just lasting a few minutes can be a helpful way to get into a mindfulness mode and to feel more alive. If part of your body is hurting, the body scan will put you in touch with those parts that are not hurting. The purpose of this is not to suppress or ignore those areas of the body that hurt, but to see them as part of a wider physical experience.

The body scan has a lot to contribute to mindfulness and even to our experience of life, even if all it does is to remind those who have forgotten that we actually have bodies. This may seem like a flippant remark but it isn't. Awareness of the body is one of the main foundations of mindfulness as outlined by the Buddha. And what is it that Christians remember most about the story of Christ? Isn't it his physical suffering? The resurrection of his body? The miracles in which he healed other people's bodies? Notice the body. Be mindful of it. This is our heritage, however fleeting it may be.

Practice
Every now and then put a little time aside just to feel a flow of awareness moving from your toes and up through your head and back again.

Walking as a mindfulness practice
Of all the specific mindfulness practices, my personal favourite is the walking meditation. I happen to enjoy walking and if you do too, you will enjoy this one. Walking meditation is also good if you are feeling a little restless or when your mind is agitated (as is walking in itself).

This mindfulness practice involves walking mindfully and slowly in a circle or back and forth, so you might not feel comfortable doing it on the street or in a public place. On the other hand, you might have no problem with that – it's up to you. I tend to do my walking meditation at home when there's nobody around except me and the dog. The dog, who believes in the importance of large quantities of rest, ignores me as soon as she realises what I am up to.

Walking meditation is as simple and as complicated as walking just for the sake of walking and holding onto your awareness of the fact that you are walking. You might try to be aware of each footstep, one heel touching the floor as another lifts, or you might coordinate your breathing with your walking. You might note sounds around you. If you are walking at home you might hear creaks in floorboards.

See how it is already getting complicated? If you try to do all these things at once, you will end up in a knot of confusion. So it is best to settle on just one or two ways to do this practice. I try to be aware of my feet against the floor and of sounds.

As with other meditations, when you realise you have drifted away in thought, just notice what you are thinking about and then return to your walking. Mindfulness of walking is, really, pure mindfulness. You may not be sitting down or watching your breath entering and leaving your nostrils, but it is a mindfulness practice despite that – and a good one. You get in a little exercise too!

Practice
Try walking mindfully, especially if you are feeling a little restless and agitated.

Touch – always here and now
When you are aware of touch you are, by definition, being mindful because awareness of touch always occurs in the here and now. If you lost all sensation of touch you would find it quite impossible to navigate your way across the room, let alone across a busy street. And yet as we go through our day and, indeed, through life, we seem to progressively forget more and more of that very important sense. Tune in right now: perhaps to the feeling of your clothes against your body, your feet against the floor, perhaps your back against your chair. If you are outside, notice the sensation of a breeze against your skin or of your feet against the surface on which you are walking.

If you are wearing shoes, what do your feet feel like where they meet the shoe leather? All of these sensations can occur outside our awareness, except when they deliver us a sharp pain, which brings them back very much into focus. Touch your partner's hand. What does it actually feel like? How long is it since you experienced that sensation with that person? When you're driving along in your car, what does the steering wheel feel like to touch?

Touch, by pulling you out of your thoughts, can help give you a sense of spaciousness in your experience. It can ground you against anxiety. If you're caught up in thoughts that make you anxious, returning to the feeling of your feet against the ground, your back against the chair and so on can give you a certain detachment from those thoughts and bring you into contact with current reality.

In other words, mindfulness of touch can change your relationship with your anxiety, so that instead of consuming you it becomes part of your experience. Mindfulness of touch can help anxious people when other methods fail and when the pull of anxiety on the mind is exceptionally strong. On a more positive note, a life lived in awareness of the touch of the things around us is a fuller life than one that is dulled to the sense of touch.

Developing the sense of touch can also help with feelings of physical discomfort. If I have discomfort in my arm, for instance, it is difficult not to be aware of that. However, if you have discomfort in your arm it is very likely that other parts of your body are free of discomfort and you reduce your preoccupation with the discomfort through bringing these other parts within your awareness.

Practice
Find as many ways as you can to cultivate awareness of touch: notice the warmth of a cup of coffee; notice your fingers touching the computer keyboard; when you wash your hands really feel the touch of the water; when you lift the glass feel the touch of the glass, feel the touch of what you eat and drink.

Three benefits of mindful eating

If you eat slowly and with awareness, you are performing a classic mindfulness exercise – but that's not all you're doing. Mindful eating brings a whole range of benefits that we rarely think about.

Mindful eating means being aware that you are eating while you are eating. In other words, you don't gobble your food so fast you hardly notice what it tastes like and you don't eat with your mind a million miles away. By definition, therefore, mindful eating means eating more slowly than would normally be the case. I don't mean painfully slowly, I just mean more slowly. Why is this helpful outside the limits of a mindfulness exercise? There are at least three ways in which mindful eating is helpful. These relate to your life in general, to diet and to mindfulness itself.

In Gestalt Therapy you are encouraged to eat your food mindfully. This is because people who gobble up their food are also apt to gobble up life experiences without making a distinction between what works for them and what doesn't. It is as though they take whatever is thrown at them and somehow they lose their autonomy to decide what they want and what they don't want. One result of this can be that the person shrinks away from life and from new experiences instead of moving forward whole-heartedly, seeking experiences that are good for them and dropping the others. Eating slowly and in awareness is a basic Gestalt Therapy exercise to help the person to regain autonomy by learning to experience, assess, 'taste' and discriminate between what works and what doesn't work.

So if you eat mindfully you are likely to take a very different approach to life than if you eat in a trance. You will learn to discriminate between the many choices life brings to you every day and you will do so with more enjoyment because you will increase your capacity to discriminate between good and bad experiences.

Dieting is a feature of the lives of millions of people all over the world. Mindful eating has a lot to offer you if you are trying to cultivate a healthy approach to food and if you are putting on more kilos than is wise. Dieting invariably involves being mindful of what you are eating and of when and how you are eating, depending on the rules of the particular dieting regime. Indeed, it is possible that what is at the heart of successful dieting regimes is mindfulness itself. The relative slowness which mindfulness brings to eating has great significance for dieters. It takes ten to twenty minutes, so far as we can figure out, for the brain to register the fact that the stomach is full. So if you gobble your food, you may get more into you in that twenty minutes than you really need in order to feel sated and full.

Slow down your eating – mindfully eating is a prime way to do this – and give the 'fullness' signal time to reach your brain. Mindfully eating a starter course will also help to bring you closer to the time that the fullness signal kicks in. So add mindfulness to your dieting practice; I think you will be pleased with the results.

As I said above, mindful eating is a valuable practice in itself. Eating mindfully gives you many opportunities a day to practice mindfulness. That is assuming that you eat three times a day – if you eat more often that's more mindfulness! Even when you're snacking you can use it as an exercise in mindfulness.

But does all this mean mindful eating must be done in some sort of grim silence? Not at all. Mindfulness can only enhance the pleasure of a meal with others. To be aware of the food, the laughter and the conversation is to truly experience the delights of eating with friends.

Practice
Integrate mindfulness into your eating and notice the benefits it brings.

Notice the light
As I write this piece, winter has ended and spring, the real spring, has arrived – an event that occurs in Ireland around the middle of February.

Yesterday, while running in the Phoenix Park, I was almost stopped short by the sight of a warm, summery light on the faraway Dublin mountains. Of course, my mind began to wander. I fell into a fantasy in which the people who live in the mountains are sitting in their summer clothes, soaking up the sun. Then I came back to reality and noticed that some of the hills still had snow on them.

Observing the effects of light can be a marvellous aid to mindfulness, especially if you live in a country where the light changes many times an hour during the day. Each time you walk down the street or the road, notice the light and its shifting effects on houses or fields. Perhaps the light looks as though it is warming up the bricks of the houses or the trees. Sometimes in the evening, the sheer beauty of the sunset sky with its golds, pinks, blues and purples can amaze you.

At night, if you are out walking, you can observe the lights in the windows of dwellings, near or far away. What sort of emotions do you feel: longing, warmth, sadness? Just notice the emotions, don't get caught up in a story about them, and then notice your breathing. If you fall into fantasies about the people inside those rooms, just take your attention back to your breathing or to the feel of your feet against the ground.

Notice the light where you live or work. In the room I use for work, the light falling from outside can sometimes cheer up the whole space, even in winter. The halogen lamp on my desk has a soft glow, a comforting glow. A light on the mantelpiece gives a sense of cosiness. If I look at light as it falls on objects, I begin to notice more about the objects, patterns I haven't paid attention to for years, perhaps, or very beautiful designs on everyday things. Look at the light falling on cups, saucers, plates, on the table, on your hand. There is so much to see: you only have to pay attention.

Practice
Learn to look at the effects of light, whether sunlight or light from lamps and other sources. Notice the emotions you experience when you do this, without getting caught up in them, and then notice your breathing.

Mindfulness of sound

What is the loudest sound you can hear right now? For me it is a clock ticking gently in the kitchen, until I start typing and then the sound of my fingers hitting the keys dominates everything else.

How about the next loudest sound? Usually, the fan on the computer is quiet and in the background, like a faraway sea, until I pay attention to it. Another sound: a tap dripping lightly or a bird chirruping every now and then? My brain would like to resolve this dilemma and will eventually send me off to the kitchen to investigate. Already my imagination has gone beyond the bare reality of the sound and brought me a picture of a bird.

I wonder how many years of meditation it would take to be able to hear the sounds without adding pictures of dripping taps or singing birds? If you work it out, let me know! Sometimes if you are sitting there using sounds as an aid to mindfulness, you can wonder if it's possible to hear the sound without linking it to an image.

To put it a better way, you can notice that when you hear a sound it is generally linked to an image and that your brain likes to link each sound to 'its' image. If necessary, it flicks through its photograph album to see what it can find. Just being aware of that process is, in itself, an excellent exercise in mindfulness. I am on the sixth floor of the apartment of a family friend in Nice. The sound of the traffic is way below, a steady hum. In the early morning, with the balcony door of our bedroom slightly open, we can hear the binmen shouting to each other far below. French binmen do not apologise for their existence! Later, when I go onto the street, traffic sounds will predominate, punctuated by snatches of conversation, the sound of buggies being wheeled along the pavement, planes flying into the nearby airport and, now and then, a wisp of birdsong.

Sounds provide an excellent basis for mindfulness. If you are listening, or if you are hearing and if you are aware that you are hearing, then you are being mindful. Listening is a continuous activity of the human brain. However, we screen out almost all the listening we do from our awareness. In psychology, this is demonstrated by the 'cocktail party effect'. Let us say, for example, you are at a cocktail party and you are chatting to someone at one side of the room. You think you are absorbed in your conversation with this person. Then you hear your name being spoken at the other end of the room and you look around. Your brain has for the entire time been monitoring the stream of sound picked up by your ears. When a piece of information as important as your name comes along, it perks up, rather like a piece of intelligence software monitoring our emails for certain keywords.

I have managed to get to this stage of my life without ever having been to a cocktail party and so, probably, have you. However, when

I worked in a very large newsroom I remember how I would immediately look up if my name was mentioned at the newsdesk, which was about seven or eight desks away from me. Clearly I didn't look up when they mentioned someone else's name, but my brain had learned through experience to put a different value on my own name. Once my brain had spotted it and alerted me I could then come out of whatever reverie I might well have been in at the time and begin to wonder what they were talking about, what they were doing with my story and so on.

To be mindful about sounds is to be mindful about experiences that you normally screen out of your awareness. What beautiful sounds have you long since screened out: birdsong, the backing music to a lyric, the voice of someone you love? Mindfulness of sounds teaches us how many of our choices are made outside our awareness, how the very decision as to where to put our attention is so often made outside our conscious awareness, as demonstrated by the 'cocktail party effect'.

Practice
Cultivate your capacity for acceptance by spending some time listening, without judgement, to sounds: other people, traffic or whatever comes to you.

Standing

Standing? Yes! Standing gets bad press: we complain about people standing around doing nothing, about being left standing, being stood up. At one time much disapproval was expended on 'corner boys': young men who stood at street corners doing nothing. Perhaps they were early practitioners of mindfulness! Whatever they were doing, they have disappeared as a phenomenon, so far as I can see, but the bad reputation of standing has persisted.

Standing can be a valuable mindfulness meditation and one from which you might learn some things about yourself. To do a mindfulness meditation of standing, you can set some time aside or you can take advantage of the next slow queue you find yourself in.

You might begin by noticing the force of gravity pulling you downwards. Notice that sense of gravity where your feet meet the ground.

Next, notice the life energy that keeps you upright. Can you feel that energy running through you like an electric current? It keeps us standing up and you can feel that energy bubbling away if you make space in your awareness for it. Without that energy, that life force, you would instantly collapse in a heap on the ground. For as long as you are alive and conscious this energy is there for you to notice and appreciate.

Again, notice your feet against the floor. If you are standing outside, can you feel a breeze? Are you standing very still or are you moving all the time in many subtle ways as you shift your weight to maintain your balance? Are you swaying ever so slightly, even so slightly that nobody else notices? This swaying is also part of maintaining your balance.

What is your head doing? Are you looking up or are you looking to one side? Is your head bowed, is it stuck out aggressively or is it balanced peacefully? As Charlotte Selver, who was a leader of the Sensory Awareness movement for many years, pointed out, we have taken in a whole range of images from books, movies and everyday talk 'prescribing where and how the head should be in a variety of circumstances'. Heroes hold their heads high and erect; characters who are up to no good may keep their heads drawn close to protect them; people afraid of being punished may look at the ground; those who wish to exude confidence throw their heads back and so on. So there is more than you think to how you hold your head.[10]

Very often, your whole history is in the way you stand. Do you stand like someone at peace with the world? Like someone at war with the world? Like someone carrying a burden of guilt? Who in your family did you get your way of standing from? There is much to explore in mindfulness of standing and I would recommend it, especially on those occasions when you have no option but to stand anyway. If you feel a little shy about doing a standing meditation, be assured that nobody will actually know you are doing it. I am not asking you to emulate the holy men in India who stand on one leg for years, just pay attention when you are standing, that's all.

Practice
Next time you find yourself standing in line or waiting for a bus or a train, just notice the pull of gravity, notice the life energy that keeps you on your feet, notice the way you are standing and how you hold your head.

Increase your pleasure through awareness

Mary looked forward to a good meal with her friends, followed by a stroll back to her apartment along a colourful and lively street on a sunny afternoon. She did indeed have a good meal with her friends, but, in fact, when she thought of it later, she realised that she had barely registered the pleasure of eating her food. She had been too caught up in conversation to notice the taste or texture. Among the dishes, what got through to her awareness were the profiteroles for dessert. They carried such a delicious shock of sugar and chocolate that they couldn't but get through! Then, on the way back to her apartment, she had to admit she had barely noticed the pleasure of walking through a colourful and sunny street as she thought about a project at work that had snagged her mind.

It is odd: we seek pleasure and sometimes even accuse ourselves of being creatures of pleasure, yet we let even our pleasures pass by in a dream. Mary isn't the only person to eat her food outside her awareness, whether that food is a fine dish in an expensive restaurant or a fine fresh cod and chips from an Italian takeaway. I'm guilty too, but wolfing it down means I lose the pleasure of eating.

I have gone through much of my life like somebody who is handed a glass of a very fine, expensive old wine but gulps it down without a thought. What a waste. I might as well have been given the cheapest wine in the supermarket. Maybe that's a metaphor for the attitude of many of us towards much of the pleasure in our lives. The pleasure of talking, of physical comfort, of walking, of driving, of music, of conversation, of reading, the awareness of all of these can so easily be swept away.

But maintaining mindfulness of pleasure adds an extraordinary richness to our lives. There are few days that hold no pleasure and many days hold many pleasures, big and small. Perhaps I can't afford to fly off to a sun-drenched island where the newness of its pleasures impresses me so much that I cannot but be aware of them, but I can certainly increase my awareness of the pleasures I enjoy here at home. And, by the way, if I did fly off to that sun-drenched island I would start losing the sharp awareness of its pleasures after three or four days, as I am sure you too have experienced. Suddenly, the vista that entranced me on day one hardly gets a glance, the trip to the restaurant becomes routine and so on (that's why winning the lottery makes little difference to people's happiness levels after the initial delight has passed, as I explain in the piece entitled 'The hedonic treadmill, a.k.a. 'the grass is always greener on the other side').

The great thing about mindfulness of pleasure is that it enables you to increase your pleasure without spending an extra cent. All you're doing is remembering to be mindful of the pleasures that already come to you in your daily life. That mindfulness brings appreciation, which, in turn, brings a deeper, richer experience of life. The Epicureans are a byword for those who put pleasure first in their lives, but the original Epicureans found their pleasures in the simplest of things; they didn't need expensive meals or exotic holidays. They distinguished between kinds of pleasure. They included the pleasure you get from doing something while you are doing it, for instance eating a meal or taking a walk. They also included the pleasure that comes from having done something enjoyable – the pleasant fullness after a meal or the sense of alertness or delicious tiredness after a walk. Mindfulness enhances your experience of either of these pleasures.

None of this means that you shouldn't anticipate a future pleasure, such as that enjoyable meal. In mindfulness, however, we see that this anticipation belongs to the present moment and we gain sufficient detachment to avoid becoming a slave to our anticipations. Within a framework of mindfulness, anticipation is not about living in the future. It is about being aware of your present pleasure at the prospect of an enjoyable meal. That's a current pleasure, not a future pleasure. It's a pleasure that exists validly even if something happens and you have to go without the meal! Similarly, the pleasure of the aftermath is not a matter of living in the past. It is an awareness of the current pleasure you feel at the experience you have had. So you will go on choosing pleasure (except during periods of deep depression when the experience of pleasure seems to be lost for the time being). But by bringing awareness to your choosing of pleasure and to your experience of it, you will greatly increase that pleasure.

You may find the awareness of pleasure harder than you expect. As Cistercian nun Miriam Pollard says in *Acceptance: Passage into Hope*,[11] 'Many of us are so incompetent at being pleased that we don't have enough genuine, simple pleasure in our lives to sacrifice if we wanted to. What we have is a superficial substitute.' Mindfulness of pleasure helps practitioners distinguish between genuine pleasures and mere habit. Watching four soaps in a row on TV every evening may be a genuine pleasure for you and good luck to you if it is; on the other hand, it may just be a habit and mindfulness might push you in the direction of new, real pleasures.

Practice
Try to notice what experiences bring you pleasure throughout the day and to maintain your awareness of them as they occur.

The hedonic treadmill, a.k.a. 'the grass is always greener on the other side'

The 'hedonic treadmill' is a great phrase thought up by psychologists to describe one aspect of our relationship with happiness. Behind the phrase is the idea that we tend to get used to the good things that come to us and so lose much of the pleasure they initially gave us. We then look for a new product or experience to increase our level of pleasure and, of course, the same thing happens again: we get a temporary boost and then we fall back to our old level of happiness/unhappiness. So we're like hamsters on treadmills, each on our own little wheel, working away dutifully to get more pleasure but always ending up back where we started.

The good news is that mindfulness can help break this cycle which so dominates our lives as commerce seeks to persuade us that the next thing and the next thing and the next thing will bring happiness. Mindfulness, as outlined earlier, can help us get more out of the pleasures we already enjoy, in the understanding that pleasures come and go. Mindfulness helps us spot the tendency, as it occurs, to abandon what we have and to hare off in pursuit of something we don't have, and then to abandon that and hare off in pursuit of something else.

The 'hedonic treadmill' applies even to lottery winners. We all think a big win on the lottery would change our lives for the better. How could it not? All that money! All those choices! Yet researchers have consistently found that people who win the lottery enjoy an early euphoria, but return to their previous levels of happiness after a year or so. Indeed, some unfortunate people find their happiness wrecked due to bad financial choices made when they were in that state of euphoria.

Mindfulness, because it is concerned with awareness of our experiences right here and now, helps us step off the hedonic treadmill. It pulls the focus away from the future. The blue sky I see through my window in Dublin today is just as attractive as the blue sky I could see through my window in six months' time if I bought an apartment in Spain. Of course I will see a blue sky more often in Spain than in Dublin, but if I am unaware of my here and now experiences, will I really notice? Or will I, after a week or so, go around hardly noticing the beautiful weather I thought would bring me happiness if only I bought an apartment in Spain?

Don't assume the hedonic treadmill is a feature only of boom times; the treadmill rolled along doggedly before the boom, which has recently ended. Changing your mono record player for a stereo would bring you happiness. Then changing the stereo for a music centre with external speakers would bring you happiness. Then throwing out your vinyl LPs and replacing them with CDs would bring you happiness, especially as CDs were indestructible (another proposition that turned out to be untrue). So we are all on the treadmill and we have been on it for a long time: buy this, then this, then this, then this if you want true happiness.

How does mindfulness help get us off the hedonic treadmill or at least slow it down to a humane pace? Mindfulness involves a non-judgemental awareness of the present moment. If you practice mindfulness and if you get lost in a fantasy about the next big thing in digital cameras, you have a better chance of spotting what you are doing and pulling yourself back to the current experience of your current digital camera. It is likely that you have not yet mastered 95 per cent of the features of your present camera and that the one you are fantasising about has even more great features you will never master.

Please note that this doesn't mean you will never buy yourself a new digital camera: it simply means you are less likely to be seduced by the 'buy the next thing and be happy' siren song of commerce and more likely to make a decision based on real needs in current circumstances.

This isn't about denial. Mindfulness in this context is about enjoying the pleasures of the moment in awareness of that fact, without having that pleasure hijacked by the marketing machine. In mindfulness we realise that a life made up of wanting, wanting, wanting is, indeed, a life spent on a treadmill. So we try to step into a different framework for our lives, one in which appreciation of the present moment becomes more important than anticipation of the future.

Mindfulness also adds value to your encounters with other people. People who adopt the philosophy of 'get the next big thing and be happy' in their personal relationships are doomed to a lifetime of wrecked relationships and a lifetime of unhappiness. To them the concept of contributing to a current relationship is less important than getting on to the next one, with the usual dismal results at the end of the day. Most of us are not on a hedonic treadmill when it comes to relationships, but those who are pay a high price, as does anyone unfortunate enough to become involved with them. For such people mindfulness can be a blessing, but I would suggest that they may need help at a deeper, therapeutic level too.

Practice
Look around you. What can you appreciate in what you have now?

Loosening the bonds

That great translator of Buddhism into Christianity and the Western tradition, Anthony de Mello SJ, liked to hammer home the lesson that we are all led by the nose by our attachments. The term refers to the things we want and need and which we feel we cannot really do without. We become attached to a reputation, a person, a pleasure and so on. In fact, we have thousands of attachments and we begin to see the world as a place that either does or does not deliver on our attachments. When we do that, we stop seeing those areas of reality that have nothing to do with our attachments. We distort our vision and even our own experience.

If I am attached to the idea that all Muslims are extreme fundamentalists, then I will especially notice news reports that confirm this view. I will discount the existence of the overwhelming majority of Muslims who just want to live, love, work and get on with their lives. If I am attached to changing my car every year, then I may well take on extra debt to meet that attachment or I may feel irritated and embarrassed because I am driving last year's car. If I am attached to having my steak well done, then a medium-rare steak could ruin my meal. If I am attached to sunshine, then even a light rain can destroy my day.

The idea that we need to break free from our attachments, or at least loosen up our connection to them, is seen nowadays as a Buddhist one, but it can be found in many traditions, of which I will say more later. In psychology, if we look at the work of Dr William Glasser, who developed Reality Therapy and Choice Theory, we see attachments addressed in terms of what he calls the

Quality World. The Quality World contains all of the things that really matter to you, that you want, that you try[12] to get and that you become frustrated about if you don't get. Indeed, Glasser describes the quality world as your own personal Shangri-La, but the thing about this Shangri-La is that when you become too attached to what it contains, you suffer frustration when you don't get it.

You could even become so attached to a particular type of pleasure that pleasure in general is denied to you. For instance, I sometimes wonder about the attachment that certain gourmets have towards food that is cooked in just the right way for them. They seem unable to enjoy a meal unless it is cooked exactly the way they want it. They set down conditions for their own enjoyment of food and are denied the wider enjoyment that can come from a more tolerant attitude to food and how it is cooked. Perhaps I am being unfair to gourmets here, but that, certainly, is how some of them come across to me.

The Epicureans, whom I mentioned earlier, were aware of this problem. They are often seen nowadays as philosophers who advocated pleasure above all things (primarily they advocated the avoidance of pain), but they warned strongly against developing attachments that cannot be satisfied. As far as they were concerned, a simple meal is something that is within the capacity of almost anybody to have. It is a desire that can be satisfied. On the other hand, a taste for very elaborate meals cooked in certain ways is something that cannot easily be satisfied and an attachment to such luxuries should, therefore, be avoided.

In the Christian tradition, the concept of self-denial can be seen in one of two ways. In a negative sense, self-denial can be an expression of hatred of 'self', of the person, and can do more harm than good. However, in a more positive sense, self-denial can be seen as a way of breaking the hold of attachments so that the person is freer to live their life in a more fulfilling manner. There is, of course, more to self-denial in Christianity than this, but I simply want to make the point that the value of loosening the hold of attachments has been put forward outside the Buddhist tradition.

Mindfulness is a primary tool for loosening those attachments. Our link to attachments is very often kept alive by thinking about them and by fantasising about them, as well as by the physical and emotional feelings we have towards them. If we can notice that thinking and fantasising are going on and if we can just let it pass on by, we can begin to loosen our dependence on the things to which we are attached. Similarly, when we notice the emotion or physical urge to do something to which we are attached, we can simply notice it.

This does not mean that we give up the things that we like. It simply means we become less attached to them. We can enjoy them in the knowledge that we will not always have them or that they are not quite the way we wanted them to be. So the practice of mindfulness helps us to work with our attachments in ways that are particularly valuable to us. It enables us to get more out of life and not be imprisoned by the frustrations of not getting the things we want, or of getting the things we want but not in the exact form we wished for.

Practice
In experiencing what is important to you, try to be mindful that, as many traditions point out, all things arise and all things pass away. Appreciate important experiences and people in that knowledge and not through the distorting lens of a 'must have' attachment.

Mindful stillness
In stillness you become yourself. You claim your autonomy. I don't mean the drugged stillness of someone hypnotised by a TV I mean an alert stillness as practised in mindfulness. You can practise stillness by sitting on a chair or a cushion and setting a period of time aside for this work. Or you can watch out for what might be called accidental opportunities for stillness. You might be sitting on a bus or a train, at your desk or in a waiting room and use this as an accidental opportunity to cultivate stillness.

In stillness you step out of the conversation in your head. You place your attention on the feeling of your body at rest. In particular,

I think it is helpful to notice your hands. Let your hands be still and just notice them. Notice their warmth. As you notice them they will almost certainly become warmer. Notice your breathing. Notice your tummy, your diaphragm as you breathe. Through this noticing you cultivate stillness.

That is all you have to do. Stillness is so simple and yet many of us fail to benefit from it. In a busy world it is even possible to feel you are doing something subversive when you practise stillness. Perhaps the stillness police will tap you on your shoulder and issue you with a fine for failing to be busy enough! Yes, stillness police do exist – mostly inside our own heads. Our own anxieties, allowed to scamper around our minds like chattering monkeys, assure us that the world will end if we practise stillness in the middle of the day.

At times we fall very naturally into stillness. People who are in love can be still with each other, look into each other's eyes for ages and find the whole experience very agreeable indeed. A parent can experience a wonderful sense of stillness holding a sleeping baby. Even crowds can be still. Think of the crowd at a football match when a crucial penalty is about to be taken. You may have experienced stillness in the theatre or at a concert. So stillness is not a strange, esoteric thing; it is your heritage. Claim it in mindfulness.

Practice
From time to time, notice opportunities for stillness. In particular, notice the stillness in your hands. Step out of the conversation in your mind to practise stillness, even if only for half a minute.

STRESS AND DISTRESS

How mindfulness improves your chances of a good night's sleep

Even mindfulness cannot guarantee a good night's sleep. However, the practice of mindfulness can help you to reduce or eliminate behaviours that contribute to keeping you awake. In this way, you boost your chances of sleeping well.

The first behaviour that keeps people awake is going over their fears and worries as they lie in bed in the dark. The trouble with this, of course, is that those fears and worries seem greater than ever during the night. In fact, they may seem terrifying and beyond our capacity to do anything about (I bet you've had that experience and so have I). The world becomes a far more threatening place. There you are, poor thing, all alone on a small, dark planet in a universe intent on crushing you. No wonder you can't sleep! So the first rule about mindfulness and sleep is this: when you spot yourself lying awake thinking about your problems, just note this fact and then focus your attention on your breathing, on the feel of the bedclothes, on your tummy moving in and out and so on. Keep returning your attention to these things.

If your mind wants to chatter, let the chatter run into the sand. For instance, if your mind says, 'Last week's sales were 10 per cent below average', just return your attention to your breathing, your tummy, etc. Don't add the next sentence, which might be, 'Yes, well, it's the middle of January and nobody has any money', just return to your breathing, your tummy. You don't want your logical mind to get going on the sales figures when you are supposed to be asleep. You want it to shut up, so don't carry on the sentence. Let it run into the sand. Needless to say, the same principle applies if your mind says, 'I think purple suits Cecilia better than yellow'. Resist the temptation to say, 'I don't know, the red she wore to the concert last Sunday wasn't bad either'. Return to your breathing, your tummy, the bedclothes. Leave Cecilia alone. Let her run into the sand.

People who find it hard to sleep often lie awake at night worrying about not sleeping. What time is it now? How much time do I have left before morning? Will I be like a zombie tomorrow? You don't need me to tell you that these thoughts generate extra anxiety and help to keep us awake for even longer. Again, with mindfulness, we can notice ourselves going into that spin of worry and instead let the thought go on by and bring our attention back to the fact that we are breathing and lying on the bed, which is nice and comfortable. We can let the sentences run into the sand, just like we did with Cecilia and the sales figures.

Let's wind back a little to the day you had before you got to your bed. When you worry a great deal during the day, when you ruminate about problems or because you are depressed, you go to your bed with a heavy load on your mind. So far as we can make out, the brain processes the day's experiences as we sleep. This seems to be a function of dreams. So when you fill your head up with a huge amount of mental activity, you leave your brain an awful lot of processing to do at night. The brain uses up about 20 per cent of the body's energy, more than any other organ. This may explain why a depressed or over-anxious person can wake up feeling tired in the mornings, even exhausted: the brain has been siphoning energy all night to help it process the day's stresses.

Practising mindfulness during the day greatly reduces the mountain of work waiting in your brain's 'in-tray' at night. By practising mindfulness during the day, of course, you can also notice yourself getting into a run of depressive or anxious thoughts: briefly note these thoughts and then bring your attention back to sounds and sights, to the feeling of your feet on the ground and to other aspects of your moment-to-moment experience. By noting your thoughts briefly and then bringing your mind back to your sensory experiences (what you see, what you hear, etc.) you can break that cycle of obsessive thinking or fretting. Breaking that cycle helps to de-stress you and, therefore, gives your brain far less work to do at night. This, in turn, increases your chances of getting a good night's sleep.

As I have said, nothing can guarantee a good night's sleep, but the practice of mindfulness can do much to substantially increase the chances that you will sleep well. Even if you don't actually fall off asleep, taking a mindfulness approach will at least enable you to get a better quality of rest than you would get if you were tossing and turning and fretting. So try using mindfulness to deal with your sleep issues – I think you will be pleasantly surprised at the outcome.

Practice
Instead of lying awake worrying at night, keep returning your attention to your breathing, the rise and fall of your tummy, the feel of your bedclothes. During the day practise mindfulness to lighten the load on your brain at night.

Panic attacks

Panic attacks come in many forms: racing heart, profuse sweating, shortness of breath, fear of fainting, a sensation of dread, a need to get out of where you are. Panic attacks can differ in their symptoms from one person to another. Symptoms can include some or all of the above and many that are not listed. Fortunately, panic attacks tend to be relatively short in duration, usually peaking in about ten minutes and then falling way. However, it is a very unpleasant ten minutes and the experience can sometimes go on for longer. No wonder people who have panic attacks become very strongly motivated to avoid them whenever possible.

The cause of panic attacks is unclear, but it is thought that the brain may misinterpret a little surge in anxiety, such as we all have from time to time. The brain spots this surge, thinks you are in danger and throws you into a panic. The purpose of the panic is to get you out of danger, which isn't much help if you aren't in danger in the first place! The fact remains, though, that panic attacks are poorly understood and all we really know about them is that they are unpleasant, irrational and generally unpredictable events.

Intense anxiety, however, is almost always a feature of these unpleasant events. It is the desire to escape that intense anxiety that leads people to change their routine so that they don't have panic attacks. A person may no longer go to the town centre or travel on trains, for instance, because of the danger of experiencing a panic attack. But panic attacks can be unpredictable and so the person who seeks to avoid them at all costs may end up confined to his or her own home.

How, then, are you to regain your freedom if you suffer from panic attacks? Remember that when you avoid panic attacks you are almost certainly avoiding having the experience of intense anxiety that comes with them. If you can gradually allow yourself to experience that anxiety, to accept it even, then the need to avoid the panic attack is greatly reduced. If you are willing to accept that anxiety, then you can go into town or shopping or travel on the train or whatever it is that the fear of panic attacks has prevented you from doing. Moreover, you may find that your panic attacks become less intense and that you have fewer of them. They may go away altogether, but this cannot be guaranteed.

Psychologist Christopher Germer[13] points out that the greater our willingness to feel, the less our anxiety. In other words, if you are prepared to feel your anxiety, then that in itself will usually lessen it.

So how would you apply a mindfulness approach to panic attacks? The strategy is to change your relationship to the anxiety that accompanies a panic attack. Begin by imagining you are having a panic attack. Notice the feelings that rise and fall. Just watch them follow their course. See how long it takes them to fade away. Next, go into one of the milder situations in which a panic attack can occur. So if the panic attack you might have on the street is milder than the one you might have on the bus, begin by going onto the street. Again, observe the symptoms rise and fall. See how long it takes for them to fade away. When you find you can experience the feelings of anxiety and panic in this situation without running away from it, go on to a more demanding situation. This is the process. If it helps, you might ask a friend to accompany you at first. Then you might ask the friend to be somewhere nearby as you go into the situation. Finally, practise going into the situation on your own. In this way, you gradually manage to tolerate the anxiety and the panic attack and to experience a wider and wider range of situations that had been cut off from you by your fear of panic attacks. Remember again that your primary purpose is not to get rid of the panic attacks, but to experience them without fear.

To sum up the mindfulness approach: observe the panic attack and its physical symptoms as you go about your business, but avoid getting into a series of conversations with yourself about how awful the panic attack is. Try to maintain a sort of silence in your head about what's going on as you observe it.

To maintain that silence or to avoid that conversation you might silently repeat, if you like, a word such as 'anxious' or 'tension', because labelling emotions has been found to help dampen them down. Using mindfulness when having a panic attack will also help to slow down your breathing. Over-breathing can make the panic attack much worse, but observing your breathing tends to slow it down.

Practice
When you feel the symptoms of a panic attack, try to observe their rise and fall without getting into a conversation in your head about it and without running away. The attack will peak in about ten minutes.

Living with emotional pain
When people experience emotional pain their first instinct is a perfectly understandable one: to get rid of it as soon as possible. Sometimes this works and sometimes it doesn't. The pain of anxiety can sometimes be alleviated by doing the things you are anxious about or by asking for help. The pain of remorse can sometimes be alleviated by asking forgiveness or by making amends. The pain of fear can sometimes be alleviated by running away.

But, as we all know, it isn't always like that. Sometimes you can't make amends. Sometimes even doing the thing that you are anxious about doesn't get rid of the anxiety. Think of the actor who has stage fright every night for an entire career. Sometimes running away doesn't get rid of the fear if whatever you are afraid of is following you. And sometimes you can't run away. You cannot, for example, run away from a serious illness.

We also have a tendency to seek distraction from emotional pain. These distractions are often linked to cravings for food, alcohol, drugs, sex and so on. As the Buddha put it, the mind, in responding to affliction, 'lights upon whatever pleasures are to be found here and there'.[14] In doing so we are, essentially, distracting ourselves by repeating old behaviours that no longer work. As Dr William Glasser has explained, each set of actions that worked for us in the past becomes an 'organised behaviour', which we tend to repeat in similar circumstances even if it doesn't work well anymore. An example of this is a person who has lost his keys and who will keep on searching his pockets long after he knows they are not there. The behaviour is ineffective, but it worked before so we reach for it again and again.[15]

Mindfulness suggests another way of dealing with emotional pain. This is not to run away but to acknowledge the pain and to allow the pain to go in its own time. If you can get rid of the pain by such simple means as doing the things you are afraid of, by making amends or by asking for help, then by all means do so – it would be foolish not to. However, I am talking about the kind of pain you can't get rid of and where the frustration of failure to end the pain can lead to drugs or drink, self-harm or even suicide, in which the person tries to get rid of pain by getting rid of himself or herself.

In mindfulness, you acknowledge that the pain is there. In so doing, you turn towards the pain instead of away from it. You allow the pain to accompany you as you do the things you need to do. Some of these things might be directly connected with that pain: getting treatment for an illness, preparing for an exam and so on. Sometimes what you are getting on with has nothing to do with the pain at all. You still need to eat, sleep, go to work, exercise and do all sorts of things that you would much prefer to do without any emotional pain, but which, unfortunately, you are now going to have to do accompanied by emotional pain.

The key factor to remember is that you do not simply stop, dwell on the emotional pain and become lost in it. Neither do you deny the pain. Instead you acknowledge its presence but you also acknowledge the presence of other things, of the things you have to do, of the people that you are with, of what you see and hear and touch as you go through your day. Your pain is part of that day, but it isn't everything that you do or everything that you experience in the day.

Given time, the intensity of pain fades. Sometimes it leaves altogether, although sometimes it does not. If you acknowledge the pain and then go on with the things you need to be doing, you will find that the pain will fade for longer and longer periods of time. But by dwelling on the pain, by engaging with it, by talking to it, that is how you keep it alive. You also keep it alive by trying to block it out with drugs or drink or by other means of escape. It is better to acknowledge the presence of the pain.

Practice
When you feel emotional pain, acknowledge its presence while you get on with your day. Don't deny it, but don't allow it to take over your whole experience either.

Staying out of the drama – mindfulness and anger

Anger can arise immediately from something that has happened just now or it can have old roots. The practice of mindfulness can help us to deal in a healthy way with the second kind of anger. If somebody pushes his or her way to the front of the queue at the post office, then no matter how diligently everybody else has been practising mindfulness, there is a good chance they will get at least a little mad!

What mindfulness helps with most is the anger that has been kept alive by constantly revisiting angry thoughts or anger, rooted in the distant past, which flows like a permanent undercurrent in the mind of the individual. Persistent thoughts of anger, whether they arise from an event that happened last week or twenty years ago, can lead anybody to lash out. By lashing out, verbally or physically, the person discharges their anger until it builds up again. Unfortunately, somebody else has to feel that lash, somebody who just happens to be in the way.

An example of this is road rage. Very often people who commit acts of road rage were angry about something completely different before they even got behind the wheel of the car. So the hapless individual who aroused their anger on the road is actually bearing the brunt of an anger that existed long before the incident happened.

Because mindfulness urges us to loosen our thoughts, to allow our thoughts to pass by, observing them but staying free of the drama they seek to pull us into, it is particularly valuable to people who are afflicted by persistent angry thoughts, and, at one time or another, I think that just might include all of us.

Sometimes angry thoughts can lead to an immediate and useful action. Sometimes they can fuel a fight for fair play. The angry thoughts I am most concerned with here are those which take on a life of their own, which disrupt the life of the person having the thoughts and which rarely offer practical or viable solutions.

In dealing with anger based on thoughts of old events, or even of very recent events, the important thing is to avoid getting caught up in the anger story again and again. Once you get caught up in re-running old scenes, perhaps having fantasy conversations in which you come out as a winner — or even in which you are martyred all over again — you are inviting anger into the home of your mind. In fact, you are inviting it to bring a suitcase and move in. Anger in the form of persistent angry thoughts is a toxic guest and sooner or later that anger is apt to explode, perhaps with the most terrible and unintended consequences.

A useful approach to persistent angry thoughts is to imagine each thought is a leaf flowing by in a stream or a bird flying away into the sky, getting smaller and smaller. An exercise like this will, in itself, give you a detachment from thoughts that can otherwise capture you and take away your peace of mind.

If you find that this isn't working, try instead to focus your mindfulness on the physical manifestations of your anger. Instead of getting caught up in the story, instead of re-running scenes in your head, notice the tightening in your chest or in your stomach, perhaps that you become physically warmer or that your breathing is harder. What you are doing here is changing your relationship with your anger. In time these physical manifestations will fade. The anger and the physical manifestations may come back from time to time, but just repeat what you have already done: notice the physical manifestations and stay out of your head.

In general, daily mindfulness practice will lessen the intensity of your anger when something happens to arouse it and will give you a valuable tool for dealing with persistent anger.

Practice

*Notice angry thoughts without getting caught up in the story they tell.
If this isn't helping, shift from your thoughts to noticing the physical manifestations of your anger, which will fade in a short time.*

Allowing resentment to blow away

When Irene decided to apply for a better job with another company, she confided her plans to a colleague whom she regarded as a friend. Without a word to Irene, her colleague applied for the job herself and got it. Six months later, Irene is still tormented by thoughts of her colleague's betrayal. She cannot get a good night's sleep for thinking about it and revenge fantasies distract her during the day.

Resentment destroys peace of mind. This is doubly so when you can do nothing about the original offence. Mentally, the sufferer endlessly recycles the offence and these thoughts call up painful emotions. Meanwhile, the offender is often blithely unaware of the dramas in the sufferer's head. If you suffer from resentment you will find that in mindfulness you can recognise that most of your emotional distress at some past wrong comes from your constant thinking about it. If you can learn to leave your resentment alone it will gradually lose energy. This understanding has freed up my emotional life and has saved me many hours of distress. Needless to say, I sometimes fail to follow my own advice. Nonetheless, a mindful approach to resentment has improved the quality of my life – of that I have no doubt.

Whenever I find myself going into resentment mode about something I cannot resolve, I remind myself that the resentment will die away if I allow it to. I then put my attention onto whatever I am doing at the time: walking, working, driving or perhaps just breathing. I may have to do this many times before the resentment fades and leaves me alone, but it's worth it.

Notice that I am not trying to pretend the original offence never happened. Neither am I trying to deny the existence of my resentment. But when it arises, I simply refuse to engage with it and instead put my attention onto whatever is going on right now. If there is some redress I can get for the original offence, a mindful attitude unclouded by resentment will enable me to see more clearly how to get that redress.

In Gestalt Therapy, resentment is seen as a demand that somebody else feel guilty, so it's not really the same as anger. Anger is about how you feel. Resentment is about how you think the other person ought to feel. However, I have little control over my own feelings, so how can I control someone else's? That is why you can get redress but go on feeling resentful if the other person seems to feel no remorse: you may be seeking what you cannot have. You need to separate resentment and redress. Resentment can only torment you and, at worst, can lead you to do something you will regret for the rest of your life.

The mindfulness approach to resentment is related to the Christian idea of forgiveness – but it differs from it too in important ways. To me, both mindfulness and forgiveness benefit the injured party. This is because the injured party is no longer caught up in thoughts of what happened in the past and is able to move forward with his or her life. But forgiveness also benefits the offender – essentially he or she is being told it is no longer necessary to feel bad about what was done. The injured party has let it go and the offender is also free to let it go, emotionally at least (the offender may be in prison with a sentence to complete).

The mindfulness approach to resentment is different. It is about allowing the thoughts of resentment and the feelings they summon to fade, regardless of whether you forgive the offender and regardless of whether you ever speak to the offender again.

But if I follow this approach of returning to my breathing or paying attention to whatever is happening around me, where does my resentment go? I can only explain this through a metaphor. Imagine that in your mind there is a cellar. In this cellar are the seeds of all the feelings you have ever had. All your joys and sorrows are down there in the cellar, slumbering. The cellar is dark. If you shine the light of attention on the seeds, they spring to life. Here is that marvellous Leonard Cohen concert you attended years and years ago – give that memory your attention and the seeds will flower into the feelings of wonder you felt at the concert. There is a cutting remark your father made about your looks when you were fifteen. Dwell on it and the hurt and anger burst into life again.

So that's where the resentment goes: it is asleep in that cellar in the dark. You can awaken it at any time by dwelling on it, but if you make a habit out of dwelling on those seeds of resentment you will pay a heavy price in emotional torment throughout your life. So you let it sleep. You let it fade into that cellar by turning your attention to your breathing or to whatever else you are doing when the resentment presents itself to you.

In the example above, Irene is tormented by memories of confiding in her 'friend', by images of her colleague sneaking off to steal the job from under Irene's nose and, perhaps even now, by images of her former colleague snug and comfortable in the job Irene wanted. Irene can do nothing about what happened so she now needs to learn, whenever these images present themselves, to turn her attention to her surroundings, to what she is doing in the present moment. Gradually that resentment will fade down into that mental cellar and she will be free to get on with her life again.

Try this approach – we all have lots of opportunities for practice!
– and see how it can help to lighten your life.

Practice
*When you feel resentful, ask yourself if there is a practical, legitimate,
viable action you can take to put matters right and consider taking it.
Whether there is or there isn't – especially if there isn't – avoid
mental re-enactments of the original offence as you go about your day.*

Anxiety and the mindfulness path of acceptance

Nobody wants to be anxious. Yet anxiety is the experience of every
human being. Naturally when we experience anxiety we would like
to get rid of it, but who has ever succeeded in entirely getting rid of
anxiety? The mindfulness approach to anxiety is to accept that you
are experiencing it, to face it, to stop running away from it. Why?
Because if anxiety is inevitable, why try running away? Moreover,
anxiety rises and falls, comes and goes. We can accept it and wait for
it to fade, as it will, though of course we know and accept that it will
come back in the future.

Some anxiety is useful. The anxiety that encourages us to provide
realistically for the future, to help our child prepare for an exam, to
give up smoking and so on, all this anxiety helps. To think of anxiety
as an ally may seem perverse, but the fact remains that rational
anxiety (unlike the irrational variety like panic attacks) gets things
done. Not that it gets any thanks!

In practising mindfulness, instead of uselessly trying to push
anxiety away, we look at it straight in the face, we notice how its
intensity changes, how it shows itself in our bodies and so on. People
often take it that anxiety means they have something wrong with
them or with their perceptions. In practising mindfulness we set that
notion aside. Anxiety is natural and normal. We seek to change our
relationship with anxiety from one of fear and avoidance to one of
acceptance.

This doesn't mean that anxiety is always 'right'. Sometimes our
anxieties prove right but very often they turn out to be wrong. I

would contend that by accepting the anxiety, by not seeking to run away from it, we are more likely to be able to see whether that anxiety has a basis in reality or not. If it does, perhaps we can do something about it – for instance, by starting to make payments on that debt we're so worried about. If it doesn't have a basis in reality, then we sit out the anxiety until it goes away of its own accord.

Here are two ideas for working mindfully with your anxiety:

MORITA: A Japanese approach called Morita Therapy, brought to the West by Dr David Reynolds[16] as a major component of his Constructive Living Theory suggests that we work with anxiety in a way which allows us to acknowledge its presence while doing what we need to do. Morita Therapy suggests a three-stage approach to getting things done:

> Know your purpose.
> Know your feelings.
> Do what needs to be done.

My purpose may be to make a presentation to colleagues at work about our new widget project. My feeling may be anxiety about whether I will seem clumsy and amateur during my presentation. What needs to be done is to prepare the presentation, stand up and make it. In other words, I don't deny my anxiety, I don't drug it out of existence. Instead I acknowledge that I am anxious and I go ahead and give my presentation anyway. I allow my anxiety to accompany my actions, if you like. So I am like the actor who allows his stagefright to accompany him while he walks out onto the stage and gets into his role.

KNOWING THE SYMPTOM: It can help also to adopt an attitude of curiosity towards anxiety, especially towards its physical manifestation. Does the anxiety tighten up areas of your body? Which areas? Does the extent of the affected area change? If you were to imagine your anxiety having a colour, what would it be? Does the colour change? How does your anxiety affect your breathing? Can you breathe softly and gently into the area affected by the anxiety? Can you feel that area softening a little?

In getting to know the symptom like this you are, in fact, changing your relationship with your anxiety. Instead of fearing it or trying to get rid of it, you are examining it. In doing so, you have taken some control over your own reactions. This approach is helpful, not only with normal anxiety but also with panic attacks.

Practice
Next time you feel anxious, notice the anxiety and accept it. See if it has anything useful to tell you about what you need to do next. Otherwise, just accept it and let it fade in its own time as you get on with doing what needs to be done.

Depression

Depression, as we are all aware, involves a descent into the gloomiest of thinking and, for this very reason, mindfulness has great benefits to offer to those who are prone to this all too common condition. There is, of course, more to depression than gloomy thoughts and we will look at that later.

In depression we take our thoughts desperately seriously, so seriously that some people are prepared to end their own lives because of these thoughts. But mindfulness changes our relationship with our thinking. Mindfulness dethrones thinking so that it no longer rules our existence. Mindfulness values all the other things that are going on in our lives and promotes awareness of these things, even if this means dropping our fascination with thinking.

Awareness of your present moment experience is painful when you are depressed, and people who are depressed are only too aware of that pain. Much of that awareness comes through thinking. This is why mindfulness of what you are physically doing and of the physical world around you can be particularly helpful when you are depressed. So try a mindfulness practice based on the physical. Are you sitting, standing, walking? What is your breathing like? What sounds do you hear? Can you just note the gloomy thoughts in your mind, as though they are just black clouds in the sky on a rainy day and keep bringing yourself back to an awareness of your surroundings, of your physical self, of your breathing?

MINDFUL WALKING. I would suggest that walking is particularly helpful to people who are depressed. Walking offers an opportunity to take your focus away from your dark thoughts. If you walk mindfully (I have included a section on mindful walking in the previous chapter, 'Body and Mind'), your mood will improve both during the walk and for some time afterwards, and this has been demonstrated many times in research. Walking in a park or the countryside or in some place that puts you in touch with nature is especially beneficial. Moreover, walking mindfully opens up the possibility of new experiences whether in observing people, places and events, or in encountering other people.

Don't be put off if the depression doesn't lift straight away. Depression is, in many ways, a mysterious condition which takes time to go. Mindfulness can help to bring closer the day that it does go and it can help you to reduce the sort of sustained, gloomy thinking that helps to prolong depression. Mindfulness can also help to reduce the chances that depression will occur again or at least it can lengthen the intervals between periods of depression.

RUMINATION IS RUINATION. The sort of thinking that is most commonly linked to depression is called rumination. That is why I like to say that rumination is ruination. Rumination means brooding on the same thoughts over and over again, going more and more deeply into them, following the thoughts not just for minutes but perhaps even for hours or days. Ruminating on gloomy judgements about yourself and about the world prolongs depression. Some psychologists speculate that women are more prone to depression because they are more likely to ruminate on their troubles. Rumination has a sort of fatal attraction to it. People sometimes seem to get a perverse satisfaction from ruminating even though it takes them deeper and deeper into depression. It may be that rumination makes you the centre of your universe or it could be that your brain becomes so used to rumination that it thinks there's something wrong if you're not doing it. If so, you need to retrain that brain and mindfulness practice will help you to do that.

Even the basic mindfulness exercise mentioned elsewhere – being aware of what you are doing, hearing, seeing and being aware of your breathing – can help you to break the cycle of rumination. Sometimes when people are ruminating they think that those thoughts are more important than anything else that might be going on in the world. I promise you that they are not. All you are doing is recycling the same old thoughts over and over again, thoughts which, frankly, are way past their use-by date. Instead, put your attention on what's happening out there in the real world, go for a walk, notice your feet on the ground, notice sounds around you, notice your breathing and so on.

Mood inspires thought. Your mood and thinking work together, sometimes to your advantage and sometimes to your disadvantage. Researchers have found that when you are in a good mood you are more likely to recall positive events from your life and to think positive thoughts about your current circumstances. Similarly, when your mood is low you are more likely to recall unhappy events and to think negatively about your current circumstances.

So thoughts and mood affect each other, but not in a simple way. Nobody can dictate what mood they will be in at any given time – if that were possible I expect we would all see to it that we were in an excellent mood all of the time, with the exception of a few dedicated masochists! So I am not claiming that you can think your way out of a bad mood. If that was possible you would have done it long ago. But it is very helpful to remember, when you are in a low mood, that the gloomy thoughts you are having are gloomy partly because of your mood and that they may help to turn that mood into a depression. When you get into a good mood – and exactly when this will happen is not in your control – your thoughts are likely to brighten.

But you don't have to be a prisoner of this process. If you are in a low mood, then in mindfulness you accept this fact. No need to panic, no need to hide away from the world. You accept that you are in a low mood, you give it time to lift and meanwhile you avoid taking your thoughts too seriously. So you use mindfulness to help you to live in the present moment, regardless of whether your thoughts are gloomy or positive, regardless of whether the experience is pleasant or unpleasant.

Mindfulness, as you can see, encourages you not to take your thoughts too seriously. Thoughts are energy in your brain. For the most part, they are made up of all the thoughts you have had before, of things people have said to you. In other words, almost all our thoughts are recycled. It's very hard to have an original thought and perhaps it's impossible to do so. So in mindfulness if you are in a poor mood and you are having sad memories you might realise, in a mindful way, that memories are just thoughts and that thoughts should not be taken particularly seriously. Far better to be mindful of the present moment which is fresh and new and has never occurred before even if you haven't left the room for a while.

THE ONLY SHOW IN TOWN? Research suggests that the more your attention is on yourself and not what's going on outside, the more likely you are to be depressed. This makes intuitive sense too. In depression, the effort required to shift attention and energy to a task outside oneself, even such a simple task like posting a letter, can feel overwhelming. Because it feels overwhelming, it is very difficult to make that shift of attention and energy when you are actually in the depths of depression. It is when you are not depressed or when you are between bouts of depression that I would encourage you to practise mindfulness of the external world, whether that is people or events or sounds or colours or smells or what you are actually doing.

This pays dividends in reducing the likelihood of depression and in lengthening the intervals between bouts of depression, but be warned: it is difficult to do if you are used to seeing yourself as the only show in town – I know!

GETTING IT DONE. Dr William Glasser emphasises that we have only limited control over our thoughts and none over our moods, but we have far more control over what we actually do. If you focus on what you do, and if what you are doing is constructive or pleasurable in a healthy way, then gradually (not immediately – don't expect it to kick in instantly) your feelings and thoughts will most likely fall in line and brighten up, even though this may take some time to happen if you are in a very deep depression. You can combine mindfulness with Reality Therapy, then, by doing some things that need to be done and by giving them your attention as best you can while staying out of your thoughts as best you can. Does the house need to be tidied? If that's too much, does the bed need to be made? Do the dishes need to be washed? Does the dog need to be walked? Do your clothes need to be brought to the laundrette? Do you need to put stuff in the washing machine? Do you need to go to the shop? Let's face it, few of us sing and dance as we do these chores. Yet doing such simple things can give you back a sense of control and can bring closer the hour when your depression lifts. When doing them, put your attention on your actions and movements and on what you actually see and hear – that's the mindfulness part.

A DEADLY TRIANGLE. People who suffer deep depressions and who recover are at risk of relapsing. Why is this? We cannot be sure. However, psychologists studying mindfulness and depression believe relapse results from a triangle of events. When people know about this triangle they can act to postpone or prevent relapse. This triangle is made up of the three major states which people experience when they are depressed: a low mood, negative thinking and fatigue. When these three are present at one and the same time, even the prospect of walking to a shop two minutes away or of getting up to answer the doorbell can seem like too much.

Sooner or later people emerge from episodes of depression. It is inevitable, however, that each person who has recovered will feel fatigue or a low mood or negative thoughts again. Why? Because we all have these experiences regardless of whether we have been depressed or not.

The person who has been depressed will, naturally, fear that the depression is back when one of these three states occurs again. And in reacting to that assumption, the person may, inadvertently, help bring the depression back. So let us suppose you wake up in the morning in a low mood. This could be due to nothing more extraordinary than a dream you have had during the night and that you have forgotten. But low mood may bring the awful, sinking feeling that the depression is back. So perhaps, in your disappointment, you stay in bed. But staying in bed until the afternoon can leave you feeling 'muggy' and fatigued. Now two of the three components of depression, low mood and fatigue, are back. From this, it takes only a second to move into negative thinking. Now you're caught in the whole triangle: negative thinking, low mood and fatigue. This, psychologists suggest, can bring you straight back into a depression.

Mindfulness practice can help to interrupt this process. First of all, if you are mindful you can notice the arrival of the first symptom or state. You can remind yourself that you are having a normal experience which does not mean your depression is back. You can still get up and go about your business while in that low mood. You know moods come and go and that, given time, this one will go too. If you are having a run of negative thoughts you can take these thoughts less seriously than before. Mindfulness teaches us to let thoughts float on by, that they are not the be-all and end-all of our existence. If you are fatigued, you can realise that this is simply a passing physical event. You can go through your day fatigued and hope to feel better tomorrow. Indeed, your fatigue may even fall away during that very day as your energy levels change. So by working with these experiences in this way, you can prevent that deadly triangle from forming and thereby greatly reduce your chances of relapse.

THE GREY ZONE. After a person has passed through a major depression, there can be a sort of grey period between the end of the depression and the return of a zest for life. It's an unpleasant period: the deep depression has gone but you are not getting a kick out of anything yet. In mindfulness it is of great importance to be aware that this grey period is a passing thing. Mindfulness will also help you to spot those little sparks of interest that signal a beginning of the return to a full engagement with life. If you spot those sparks of interest you can acknowledge and appreciate them and bring closer the day when you will feel good again.

Practice

When you are between bouts of depression, practise mindfulness. This will help you to lengthen out the intervals. It will also help you notice when you are feeling low in mood or fatigued or thinking negatively. Spotting this, you can get on with your day mindfully, thereby reducing the chances that you will slip into depression. When you are in depression, practise mindfulness of walking, of sitting, of standing, of sounds. Use this to help you break the cycle of rumination and of thinking negatively, which keeps people depressed.

Recession – living through anxious times

As this is written, the world economy is in crisis. Prophets of doom proliferate on TV screens, the internet, the radio and in newspapers. They are having a field day. Repent, they say, the end is nigh – actually, some of them say, don't bother repenting, it's too late, you're all going to be swallowed up by a great black cloud: all is lost!

Even if the crisis has passed by the time you read this (I hope it didn't last too long!) you may be experiencing your own economic crisis. Uncertainty exists in good economic times too – not every industry does well, not everybody earns big money. For some people, gloomy forecasts come true. Their jobs go, perhaps their homes are under threat or their pension plans lose money. Others still have everything they had before the crisis hit but they are afraid of the future.

Mindfulness does not make hard times go away but it can certainly help us to get through them in better shape. Mindfulness helps, not by magically changing objective facts but by enabling the practitioner to stop generating extra upset to add to the upset that is inevitably part of a crisis. Making one's reaction to a crisis worse than necessary is done by 'catastrophising', a word first used, so far as I know, by Dr Albert Ellis, who developed Rational Emotional Behaviour Therapy. 'Catastrophising' means going over and over the gloomiest possibilities of what might happen in the future, exaggerating them and then, for good measure, exaggerating them still more.

This is the opposite to the mindfulness way of putting your attention on your present moment experience and noting your thoughts without getting caught up in the dramas they present. Catastrophising can make current emotional experience worse than it needs to be. It can throw a person into a depression or into a blizzard of anxiety. Moreover, catastrophising makes it very difficult to plan for the future. Developing a good plan involves taking a clear look at resources and possibilities. The person who is caught up in a terrifying mental drama finds it hard to do this. Catastrophising makes it next to impossible to see clearly.

By returning to the present moment and by using awareness and acceptance, the mindful person can avoid getting carried away by a spiral of catastrophising that has so little to offer and that can do so much damage.

Note I am not suggesting that you will be floating around on Cloud Nine if you practise mindfulness in tough times. You will experience the degree of anxiety that is inherent in your situation. But you will experience only that, without piling anxiety upon anxiety by generating unhelpful and frightening thoughts. That, in turn, will help you to enjoy what you have now and to make good plans for the future – a worthwhile prize in good times and bad.

Practice

In difficult economic or political times, use mindfulness to help you avoid pointless and harmful catastrophising.

From the cellar – memory and mindfulness

Imagine being told you will spend the rest of your life in a dark cellar. No more sunlight for you. No more experiences out in the wide world. From now on, your cellar will be your life. Who put you into the cellar? You did, by dwelling not just *on* the past but *in* the past. Let's look at the cellar in a little more detail and then let's look at how mindfulness can help you to stay out of it.

Suppose everything you have done in the past, and everything that has been done to you, has left behind certain memories. These are not just visual memories like pictures on the page. They are emotional memories. They carry a charge. A memory might stir anger, contempt, shame, pride, resentment, admiration and so on. But where are these memories? They are certainly not in your awareness all the time or you would find it very difficult indeed to get through an ordinary day. The memories are somewhere. Somehow they or their traces exist in a form in which they are capable of being re-experienced emotionally. This must be so because otherwise you would not have emotional memories.

Now, back to the cellar. If you want to store seeds for sowing in the spring, it's a good idea to store them in a dark place so that the sunlight doesn't fool them into imagining too early that spring has come. Light brings the seeds to life, so they are kept in the dark until it's time for them to grow.

So let's imagine that you have in your mind a cellar, a store. The Buddhists call this the '*alaya*'. In this cellar are your emotional memories. They are in the dark, slumbering. But when a light shines on them for long enough, the memories come to life. In other words, you recall the memories and experience an emotional impact.

But what is that light? The light is attention. If you give your sustained attention to a memory it will come to life with its associated emotions. If the memory and emotions are positive, that's just fine. You can bask again in the reflected glow of emotions from your good experiences of the past. (Though beware of becoming a 'good memory' bore like an old soldier recalling his campaigns!)

However, all too often, as you know, the memories that we bring back to life are the dark ones, the resentments, the injustices, the embarrassments. It's as though we take a light and shine it on our most painful memories, which then spring to life. We get caught by them and we cannot let go. That's how people end up spending their days rummaging around in a cellar. They just cannot let go of attending to bad memories, especially resentments, and these memories then shape their experience of life and deny them much of the pleasure of life. There is more on resentment elsewhere ('Allowing resentment to blow away' in this chapter), but there are other seeds in that cellar, of loss, grief, anger, envy and so on, and they are all capable of being re-awoken.

If a memory has gone utterly and completely, we can think of it as not being in the cellar at all – many daily memories and many of our memories from our first five years or so are lost. The loss of early memories may be due to the massive reorganisation of the brain during those years. What we are concerned with here are the emotional memories that stay.

Let's take a look now at what mindfulness has to do with all this. We've been talking about a cellar and about rummaging around in the dark with a flashlight, which we shine on the seeds. In purely agricultural terms I am getting out of my depth here – so, out of the cellar!

Above the cellar is a daylight world. Think of this as the world of mindfulness. In this world you are concerned with experiencing the present and perhaps with making plans for the future (and remember that making plans, as opposed to fantasising, is a present moment activity). While you are mindful, two things are happening. First you are out of the cellar and in the world of the here and now, which is, usually, a better place to be.

Second, if you begin to fall into the cellar by awakening painful memories, you can see yourself doing this. You can then make a choice as to whether to continue on with that painful memory or whether to let it go.

I do not advocate that memories be repressed, pushed away or shoved out of sight. Sometimes it is important to be able to experience a memory in order to deal with the emotional aftermath of what happened. However, with many hurtful memories we make the mistake of continuing to engage with the memory long after there is any point in doing so. At worst this can lead us to see life through a lens of hurt.

In mindfulness, when you spot the memory arising, you simply acknowledge it and bring your attention back gently to whatever it is you are doing at the present moment. The memory will probably stay around for a while, but if you get on with what you are doing and if you don't start indulging it and telling yourself stories about it, then it will gradually fade back into the cellar.

A useful meditator's trick to help you with this is to label the memory. For example, say the memory is of someone cheating you out of a deserved promotion at work. Whenever you notice the memory arising, you say to yourself 'resentment' and go on with what you are doing. Or perhaps the memory is one of embarrassment at the time you left your fly open when giving a speech at the Rotary dinner. In that case you say 'embarrassed' to yourself when the memory returns. Then get on with what you are doing.

Labelling emotions has been found, in the laboratory, to dampen their effect by activating other areas of the brain. Meditators discovered this a couple of thousand years ago, but science has at last caught up!

Mindfulness allows a space in which experiences other than memory can arise. In other words, you don't become flooded by the memory — you can allow space for your normal daily experiences and interactions. In this sense, mindfulness is particularly helpful in dealing with memories that could otherwise take over your life.

The issue of memory, especially of emotional memories, provides a particularly good example of the way in which so much of your experience of life can be the creation of your mind. If you spend your time going over old resentments and old griefs you will have a very different life to what you will have if you manage to give your attention to experiences of the present.

Old memories cloud our encounters with other people. I wonder if you've ever met somebody when you were full of resentment at something they said or did last week, only to discover that they have no memory of it at all and have no idea what it is that you are going on about? I expect you have and if you haven't, then, believe me, I've done it on your behalf! A mindfulness approach at least can keep these memories in their place and can allow your experience of the person in the present moment to be based on how they are now as well as how they have been in the past.

Practice

When you spot yourself dwelling on painful memories you can do nothing about, turn your attention to your here and now experiences and gradually the memory will fade.

Two kinds of suffering: primary and secondary

To understand the mindfulness approach to pain and distress, it is helpful also to understand the concepts of primary and secondary suffering. If my wife asks me to hang a picture and if in doing so I hit my thumb with a hammer, there is a very good chance that I will jump up and down, swear blue murder and so on. I am experiencing primary suffering, i.e. the pain that inevitably goes with whacking your thumb with a hammer.

Let us say that an hour later there is still an ache in my thumb and that two hours later my thumb is sensitive and turning black. That is also primary suffering. But suppose I am also whinging about my wife wanting me to hang a picture, about the lousy hammer and the lousy nail and the lousy wall, then I am generating secondary suffering. I am adding my own specially manufactured suffering to the inevitable pain.

A less painful example might concern the weather. It's one thing to be looking out on pouring rain at the height of summer, but it's another thing altogether to spend your day complaining about the rain. Being confined indoors due to rain might be called primary suffering. Lamenting endlessly about it is secondary suffering – it is the extra suffering we add on ourselves.

Mindfulness doesn't take away primary suffering – you cannot escape primary suffering, it comes with the franchise – but mindfulness helps you to spot yourself generating secondary suffering and to drop it. People with chronic pain benefit greatly from learning the distinction between primary and secondary suffering and there is more on this in the next section.

To repeat: mindfulness doesn't make chronic pain go away, but it can help the sufferer to reduce or drop the secondary stresses that arise in reaction to the pain. It can help the person with the pain to take back a measure of control over his or her life.

A person subjected to bullying or derision can also gain a great deal from the mindful approach to primary and secondary suffering. Bullying and derision are hurtful in themselves – that's the primary suffering. But as I explain elsewhere ('Bully at work' in 'Hustle and Bustle'), the secondary suffering is what sometimes does most harm. In this case, the secondary suffering consists of obsessing about the bullying night and day, perhaps eating too little or drinking too much. By practising mindfulness, the person who is bullied can minimise the suffering that arises from this distressing situation.

Understanding primary and secondary suffering can also help, for example, somebody who feels cheated by a shop, by another person or by an organisation. Again the experience brings with it a certain amount of unavoidable suffering, but if there is nothing you can do about it – or even if there is – you need to be careful about adding extra suffering, perhaps in the form of bitterness, to the experience. Why? Because such bitterness can destroy your happiness without contributing anything to a resolution of the issue if it can be resolved. Again, mindfulness can help you spot this process happening and turn your attention to the many other things in your life.

You can see from this, then, that in helping to eliminate secondary suffering, mindfulness provides a great benefit to human beings. Secondary suffering can go on for years, even decades if a person is not aware of the distinction between the two kinds of suffering. Similarly, the suffering can go on indefinitely if a person lacks the tools with which to reduce or eliminate secondary suffering. Mindfulness is such a tool.

Practice
When something bad happens, be willing to experience the inevitable suffering that goes with it. Through mindfulness, avoid adding extra suffering.

Chronic pain and mindfulness

People in pain can be said to suffer from two types of pain. The first is the pain which arises from their injury or illness. The second is the emotional distress which they feel because of the existence of the physical pain. This emotional distress can include fear, anxiety, helplessness and panic. It is this second type of pain that meditation can help to reduce.

Mindfulness is used by many people suffering from chronic pain. Its use by people in pain has been developed by Dr Jon Kabat-Zinn of the University of Massachusetts Medical School. His approach, known as Mindfulness-Based Stress Reduction, is used in hospitals and pain clinics around the world. If you suffer from chronic pain I would urge you to read his book, *Full Catastrophe Living*.[17]

As stated above, mindfulness does not take away physical pain. It can, however, greatly reduce the emotional distress you may feel about pain. It is not a substitute for medical treatment, physiotherapy or other mainstream interventions. Think of mindfulness as an additional tool to bring to your experience of coping with pain.

One person who suffers from chronic back problems told me the use of mindfulness had given her back her life. What she meant was that the pain, though still there, was no longer the consuming focus of her attention. She was able to put her attention onto other important aspects of her life as well. That, essentially, is the mindfulness approach.

As you know, mindfulness involves becoming aware of what is actually going on right now without getting 'lost' in your imagination. For instance, you can become aware of your breathing and this is a very good way to maintain mindfulness. You can become aware of the fact that you are sitting down or lying down. If you are sweeping the floor you can simply be aware of that fact. Here is a four-part exercise to help you to use mindfulness as a response to pain (if the pain is too intense, skip Part 2):

I.

Notice your breathing.

Notice your posture.

Notice the points of contact between your body and the chair, floor, ground.

Notice your clothes touching your body.

Every time you drift into thinking, just return to noticing your breathing.

2.

If you feel pain, notice the pain without getting involved in thoughts about it. Imagine yourself relaxing into the pain with awareness.

Notice how the intensity of pain rises and falls but rarely stays the same. Again, imagine yourself relaxing into the pain with awareness.

Notice that the area of your body covered by pain will also change from time to time. And again, imagine yourself relaxing into the pain with awareness.

3.

Notice the area of your body that surrounds the area of pain. Notice how that area is tensed up. Imagine that you are breathing into that area and allowing it to relax.

Notice that there are parts of your body which have no pain. Breathe into those areas and allow them to relax.

4.

Now, as well as your body, notice the room you are in.

Notice that the room is not in pain. Notice how your pain is part of your experience but it is not your total experience.

Now notice your breathing again.

Practice

You can do this mindfulness exercise many times a day and in bed at night. It should enable you to broaden your experience beyond your pain. You can also use the many other mindfulness exercises in this book to broaden your perception and to gain a sense of spaciousness, which pain all too often takes away.

Deep injustice

Deep injustice has hurt the lives of millions: war, famine, institutional abuse, family abuse, murder – the sources are myriad. In recent times, details of the abuse of children in institutions over decades have generated disgust, anger and sadness, especially since so many continue to suffer the effects of what was done to them.

What has mindfulness to offer if you have suffered deep injustice? Mindfulness cannot take away the pain, nor can it take away the anger people feel when their lives are affected by injustice. It may not be desirable to take that anger away – anger can fuel demands for justice. What mindfulness can do, though, is change your relationship with the pain and with the feelings that stem from what was done to you. Mindfulness does not seek to deny injustice or pain or emotions. It seeks to change your relationship with these in the interest of your well-being.

Abuse (I am using this word to describe all the forms of injustice mentioned above) leaves physical and emotional effects, sometimes mingled in such a way that they are impossible to separate. One person may suffer physical pain decades after the abuse; another may have emotional pain; another may have both. Still others may have blanked out feelings in certain areas to avoid overwhelming emotional pain.

How can mindfulness help if you have been affected in any of these ways? Mindfulness of physical pain and tension can give you control over your own response to that pain and tension. It can broaden your choices. If you are able to allow pain and tension to be there without a desperate need to get rid of it, then you immediately expand the choices available to you in your life. This is especially so if you can do the things that you need to do even while you have pain and tension. (Of course, you should seek medical treatment where appropriate, but mindfulness can be a powerful ally of medicine.)

So you might practise experiencing the pain and tension in as calm a way as you can, perhaps by also being aware of your breathing, by being aware of those parts of your body that are not in pain and even by being aware of those parts of the room and the space around you that are not in pain. This is one way to begin to change your relationship to the effects of trauma (there is more on this in the section 'Chronic pain and mindfulness').

If you have been traumatised you may find that mindfulness of physical sensations brings on feelings of fear or panic. If that is so, I suggest you practise mindfulness of what is going on in the present moment outside your body: sounds, colours, the movement of leaves, light and shadow. Mindfulness of walking might suit you better than mindfulness of breathing (see 'Walking as a mindfulness practice' in the chapter 'Body and Mind'). Or you might identify those areas of your body where you do not feel the panic or the pain and be mindful of those areas. If you find mindfulness practice brings up a lot of painful memories and emotions, I would also suggest that you attend a counsellor to deal with these. If mindfulness practice has this effect then you are getting a signal that you have issues with which you need some help.

If mindfulness of breathing brings up a sense of anxiety, try breathing reasonably steadily, reasonably shallowly, not gulping your breath, but doing it with an awareness of the whole world outside of your breathing and of that space outside your breathing. All of this can help you to work with the tensions that awareness of breathing can bring up in traumatised persons. As I mentioned earlier, you may also notice that certain parts of your body are numb and, again, it can be helpful just to bring your awareness to those parts now and then and just let your awareness rest there. That awareness may ultimately help to bring you back into relationship with parts of your body that you have 'cut off' because of feelings you didn't want to have. (If you tend to have panic attacks, look up the section 'Panic attacks' earlier in this chapter.)

Sometimes emotions come through very strongly in the person who has been traumatised. The most obvious are emotions connected with loss, fear and anger. Remember that emotions are not within our direct control. You cannot directly decide that you're not going to have unpleasant emotions. That is why people who are afraid of their emotions can end up drinking or taking drugs in order to get away from them.

In mindfulness, simply observe the emotion as it arises, as it becomes stronger, as it peaks, and then observe it as it dies away again. This all helps to convince your mind at an important level that the emotion will come and go, but it will not stick at the same intensity all the time. This changes your relationship to your emotions in a healthy way.

You can experiment with experiencing strong emotions physically without getting into a series of thoughts about them. An example might be a strong emotion made up of a mix of anger, loss and a sense of injustice done to you. Constantly re-imagining what was done, fantasising about how you might have fixed it or indulging in revenge fantasies will usually worsen your emotions and, indeed, can become a mental prison. An alternative is to experience the emotion physically, perhaps noticing the tension in your chest or stomach, the change in your breathing, even in your body temperature. Notice these physical manifestations as they rise and then fall again. Do so without getting into a mental conversation or mental story about it. Again, this changes your relationship to painful emotions in a way that increases your control over your own life.

In some people, sometimes, the feelings connected with the original traumatic event hit with full force. It is as though they are living the traumatic event all over again in an emotional sense. Once again, I would strongly suggest that a mindfulness approach of calmly breathing, not gulping air and observing these sensations as they rise and fall can be of great help. Indeed, such mindful observation can help your brain move its memory of the event from what I would call its alarm centre – the fight or flight centre – into the 'historical memory' part of your brain. Every traumatic experience, when it happens, activates that alarm centre in the brain. The alarm centre instantly tells us to fight the threat or flee from it.

Once that traumatic experience has passed, the memory should become part of our historical memory. But if it gets stuck in the alarm centre, then we can be thrown into that panicky, frightening fight or flight response again and again. If you can learn to observe these sensations calmly and mindfully, then, in time, the memory can move from the alarm centre and into your historical memory. There the memory can still hurt if you dwell on it, but it will no longer overwhelm you or throw you into a panic.

Thoughts of injustice and wondering how any human being could have done this to you may also come to you often and strongly. If these thoughts can be translated into action to redress the wrong that was done, then they can be powerful indeed (see 'How mindfulness makes for better planning' in the chapter 'Hustle and Bustle'). But thoughts that sweep you away and torment you can ruin your happiness without achieving anything to redress the original wrong. In mindfulness, you can learn to observe the fact that you are having a thought, allow the thought simply to be there and let it pass in its own time.

Mindfulness is especially valuable in helping to break cycles of thinking in which the same thoughts are recycled over and over and over again without ever coming to any conclusion. Just observing the thoughts as they rise and fall, and allowing them to take their own course without getting caught up in them, can be a great relief to people affected by cycles of distressing thoughts.

If you have suffered deep injustice then you are well aware of how that injustice can go on hurting you through painful thoughts and emotions. Mindfulness does not seek, as I said above, to take away your anger at what was done or your desire for justice. What it does is help you to make the best of your life and your relationships without allowing the injustice to limit your whole life.

Practice
Use the exercises and approaches mentioned here and in the rest of the book to help free you from the shackles of deep injustices done to you.

ENCOUNTERS

What about me? Mindfulness, the self and relationships

Mindfulness loosens the preoccupation with the self. Why is this a good thing?

First, many of us are in pain because of our attempts to placate or glorify the self, because of shame about the self, because of attempts to make the self perfect or because of the disruptive effect of attempts – such as panic attacks – to protect the self. Am I good enough? Who do I think I am? Questions of this sort all arise from our preoccupation with the self. They can form part of a process of beating ourselves up over mannerisms, ways of talking, even ways of thinking. If we can loosen up that preoccupation even a little, we can feel freer and our relationships with other people can improve.

SELF AND RELATIONSHIPS: Excessive preoccupation with self disrupts relationships. At the extreme end of the scale, a narcissist can be so involved with self that he or she is incapable of placing a value on the needs of other people. Equally, a person with a huge sense of entitlement may utterly distort his or her perception of other people. Everyone and everything is seen as fitting in or not fitting in with that sense of entitlement. Their commitment to the 'self' is so great that others cannot maintain satisfying relationships with them. Others may stay with them because they place a low value on themselves or for the sake of the children, but the relationship is very likely to be one of pain for the partner of such persons.

PUTTING ATTENTION OUTSIDE THE SELF: Mindfulness helps you see that you are not simply an individual alone in the world or around whom the world revolves. You are somebody's friend, somebody's parent, somebody's child, somebody's partner, somebody's neighbour. Mindfulness helps the practitioner to see the importance of rebalancing one's priorities away from a preoccupation with a 'self' that must be appeased and towards a wider social experience.

Certain Japanese approaches, such as Morita Therapy, emphasise the importance of placing one's attention on what is external to the self. In this approach we are encouraged to harmonise our attitudes with the universe – to accept things as they are. Thus, cleaning your room, gardening or doing a piece of necessary work are all seen as more important and beneficial than agonising about the tendency of the universe to get out of step with one's own wishes!

In this regard, the British mental health organisation, Mind, found that 90 per cent of people who took an outdoor walk in a country park reported a boost in their self-esteem. Of those who were depressed, 71 per cent reported an improvement in their mood. Of people suffering from tension, 71 per cent felt better after a walk in the park. That is a telling example of the benefits of putting your attention outside yourself and onto the external world. By contrast, Mind found that the benefits of walking in a shopping centre were very limited, but then a shopping centre is all about 'me, me, me' – what's here that I'm interested in buying? So here again the non-self approach is vindicated.[18]

SELF AND CONTRITION: Loosening up the self also allows us to be contrite when we have done wrong. Instead of rushing to protect our self-esteem by denying all wrong-doing, we can acknowledge, at least to ourselves, what we have done and, if possible, make amends. Contrition allows us to break out of the prison of the self.

Philip Zimbardo, in his work on evil, even suggests that developing a sense of contrition is a protection against perpetrating torture, murder and other evil acts against other people.[19] An excessive preoccupation with the self stands in the way of contrition. Mindfulness opens up the way by loosening that preoccupation.

Practice

Practising mindfulness of your thoughts and emotions is valuable, but try also to cultivate mindfulness of the world outside yourself: people, sights, sounds and so on.

Relationships and mindfulness – keeping a fresh, authentic view

If mindfulness isn't helping to improve your relationships, then you're probably doing it wrong. And if it's harming your relationships, for instance if people close to you complain that you have withdrawn, then you are definitely doing it wrong.

Mindfulness is about maintaining deliberate awareness of your present, ongoing experience. Therefore, the practice of mindfulness should help keep good relationships fresh and it should help you to see more clearly if a relationship is unhealthy.

Relationships are so easily shaped by our tendency to label experience and then see the label and not the person. I may label a person as friendly and fun on the basis of experience. My attitudes towards him are positive and I enjoy socialising with him. Suppose one night he gets drunk and shows a dark side to his character. Now the label changes. When I meet him again I 'see' a different person. The drunken behaviour may have been what we call 'out of character', but that is what I see when I next look at the person.

Another way to put it is that the power of habit is so great that in long-term relationships especially, we can so easily stop seeing the person who is in front of us. We can almost discount their presence in the room.

Sometimes we see people through a distorting lens of old resentments. Whenever we notice them we think at some level of all the annoying or outrageous things they have done, even years ago. They might as well be going through life wearing sandwich boards advertising their sins!

Or we can see a person through a lens of positive illusions – rose-tinted spectacles. An example might be the parent who sees one of his or her adult children as a golden boy or girl who can do no wrong. This person may be exploiting the parent financially or may be ignoring the parent's health and emotional needs. Another child may, in fact, be doing far more to help the parent. However, the golden boy or girl continues to be seen as, well, golden, thanks to that lens of positive illusions – very frustrating for everyone else!

In the hurly burly of raising children, too, it is so easy to lose sight of the positive aspects of the experience. Mindfulness can help us to see this happening and to bring us back to an appreciation of our children. Mindfulness, in other words, can help us see through our habitual reactions. This is a most valuable benefit of the practice of mindfulness. Old routines, old habitual perceptions all too often govern relationships.

And it's not only old routines that govern relationships. Many reactions occur in a sort of haze: you get angry so I get angry; you're bubbly so I'm bubbly; you remind me of an aunt I didn't really like so I'm giving you a hard time, although I don't really know why I am; and so on.

This has huge implications for our relationships. In mindfulness we have some hope of cutting through the haze, of seeing clearly. We can still make idiots of ourselves, we can still have relationship problems – perfection is not an option – but at least in mindfulness we can see ourselves starting to make idiots of ourselves and now and then we can stop in time!

Practice
Try to maintain a mindfulness approach in your encounters with other people. Notice the extent to which, perhaps, you are no longer seeing the real person and let mindfulness give you a fresh view.

Parenting
It is, I think, fairly well known that the pressures of parenting, especially of small children, can leave adults demented from time to time! Can mindfulness help mums and dads keep their sanity? I believe it can – though stress-free parenting has yet to be invented.

Quite apart from the question of keeping your cool under pressure, there's the more important issue of what you miss as a parent if you are constantly swept away by screaming fits and other negative emotions. Small children are very good at pressing your buttons. They know just what to do to get you going. Why wouldn't they? They have been studying you intently ever since they were born. What's more, they have inherited many of your traits, including, presumably, the maddening ones.

So parents who let small children push their buttons and who react by flying off the handle are doomed to continue flying off the handle for many years. This will do no good at all to the parents' health or peace of mind and it isn't much fun for the children either. In the cut and thrust of getting through the day or getting through the current row, it can be very easy to forget what a blessing this child is and what a blessing it is to be in a position to rear this child.

Research suggests that the happiness level of parents falls almost as soon as the first child is born and doesn't begin to rise substantially until the last child leaves home. I think this research misses a point, which is that we don't have children in order to be in a state of bliss all the time. We raise children because they fulfil a very deep need in ourselves. The experience of parenting helps to fulfil that need. It reaches out to something very instinctive in us. Indeed, even if you look at people who don't have children but have favourite nephews or nieces on whom to lavish their generosity, you can appreciate the strength of the need to nurture a new generation.

Of course, sometimes anger with your children is appropriate and you can't be popular all the time. In fact, there are stages of your child's life when you might not be popular any of the time. That change is usually a characteristic of the teenage years and it usually passes – honest!

What you want to avoid is losing your head senselessly and in ways you will later regret. For instance, if your child refuses to sit down and eat her dinner and if roaring and screaming doesn't change her mind, then roaring and screaming is a complete waste of time and will achieve nothing beyond making you lose your appetite in the process. To deal with the situation (and this is not a parenting book so I'm not getting into that here), you need to keep a cool head. To do this, use some basic mindfulness techniques when interacting with your children in fraught situations:

– Stay aware of your breathing to anchor your mind and emotions.
– Learn to be aware of the physical manifestations of anger and frustration without getting into a rush of thoughts about it in your head.

Gradually, you will gain more control over yourself and over the situation. Of course, you might deliberately put on a display of anger at certain times and at times that might be appropriate. What I'm talking about here is not getting totally swept away willy-nilly by whomever happens to press your buttons next. By taking a mindful approach to interactions with children you can greatly reduce the dangers of such button-pushing happening and you can greatly improve your relationship with your children. Moreover, you can improve your own sanity and you can appreciate the very great gifts that they bring you.

Practice
Stay in touch with your breathing to preserve your presence of mind in fraught interactions with your children.

Spirituality and mindfulness

Is mindfulness a spiritual practice? Some would say no, others yes. In his work with people suffering chronic pain and stress, Jon Kabat-Zinn uses what you might call a non-spiritual approach to mindfulness. Such an approach is consistent with the nature of the work he does at the University of Massachusetts Medical School. In helping people of all faiths and none, he is, I think, wise to leave the question of spirituality to themselves.

On the other hand, Anthony de Mello SJ, who interpreted mindfulness to the world many years earlier, was a profoundly spiritual man, though his expression of spirituality was more robust than most of us are used to. He had a personality that bubbled with enthusiasm and energy and he loved to challenge, as anyone can tell when watching videos of his presentations or reading his books. It seems to me that mindfulness can be adopted as an entirely secular practice or as a spiritual practice.

Here are some ways in which I believe mindfulness and spirituality can converge:

1. 'BE STILL AND KNOW THAT I AM GOD.' This admonition from Psalm 46 is taken by many people as a phrase for meditation and prayer. To be still and to rest in an awareness of God is itself a form of mindfulness. Similarly, the use of this phrase, its use as a mantra or prayer in itself, is both an act of mindfulness and of spirituality.

2. CONTEMPLATION OF CREATION AS THE WORK OF GOD. Those who contemplate the world around them as the work of God and who seek to remain in the awareness of their contemplation are engaging in mindfulness. At the same time, the contemplation of the world as the work of God is a deeply spiritual act.

3. CONNECTEDNESS. Mindfulness almost always leads to a sense of connectedness with people, with the world, with other persons practising mindfulness. Connectedness is also seen by many as a form of spirituality whether that sense of connectedness is derived from prayer, shared experiences or being with people you love. By enhancing that sense of connectedness, mindfulness can enhance one's spiritual experience.

4. APPRECIATION OF A WIDER REALITY. Both spirituality and mindfulness lessen the importance of the self by cultivating an appreciation of a wider reality. In mindfulness, we begin to see the self as made up of habits, attitudes and unexamined assumptions. In spirituality, the sense of a greater presence, of being part of something we cannot comprehend also diminishes the notion of the self as the be-all and end-all of existence.

5. PRAYER. To pray in mindfulness seems to me to be a more spiritual experience than racing through a prayer, wishing it was over and thinking about what you are going to do next. Indeed, I'm not sure the rushed version has anything to do with spirituality at all. Add mindfulness and the act of praying becomes a spiritual experience.

6. WHAT QUALITY? Many of the mindfulness practices in this book, such as asking, 'What quality am I bringing to this moment?' can be seen as having a spiritual dimension because they emphasise that there is a relationship between you and your immediate experience and that you have some responsibility for that relationship. Such a relationship can be seen as a spiritual one or as including spirituality. Indeed, such a practice can be deliberately engaged in as an act of spirituality.

7. FAITH. It seems to me that faith, in itself, can be a mindful act. Faith very often is unexamined, unquestioned. But for those who say, 'I have faith even though I do not know', faith is a choice made in awareness and mindfulness is awareness. Such a faith, I would suggest, is stronger than the unexamined variety.

8. WORK AS WORSHIP. Those who see their work as an act of worship or as a spiritual act are likely to do that work with awareness of its significance to them. Such an awareness can only be improved by the practice of mindfulness.

These are just some ways in which mindfulness and spirituality can converge. Whether your spirituality is religious or secular in nature, I believe mindfulness can deepen the spiritual experience.

Practice
If you have a spiritual practice, consider the ways in which it can converge with or be enhanced by a mindfulness practice.

MINDFULNESS IN SPORTS

Mindfulness: essential sports equipment

Mindfulness has been used by many sports stars throughout the world: Tiger Woods (golf star), Apolo Ohno (speed skater and US Olympic Gold Medalist), Phil Jackson (basketball coach with the Chicago Bulls and, later, the Los Angeles Lakers). In Ireland, sports psychologist Felicity Heathcote was teaching mindful breathing techniques to Irish Olympic athletes in the late 1970s and her contribution to the Irish performance in the 1992 Barcelona Olympics has been highly praised (she has written about her work in *Peak Performance – Zen and the Sporting Zone*).[20] Mindfulness, the awareness of what you are experiencing right now, is essential to the performance of sports. It doesn't help in sports to be lost in your imagination and completely unaware of what you are doing!

Yet people playing sports, whether team sports or solitary sports, can get caught up in all sorts of distractions that can prevent them from achieving their best. These distractions include:

> Criticising yourself for the mistake you've just made.
> Worrying about the opposition.
> Worrying about looking foolish.
> Fantasising about winning.
> Fantasising about losing.
> Re-living a foul that an opponent just carried out on you.

The first value of mindfulness in sport is to clear your head of these distractions. The second is to bring you to a state of sufficient detachment and flow, to be able to perform better at what you are doing.

Here are some thoughts on mindfulness and sporting performance:

1. AWARENESS OF THE FULL BODY. Notice your whole body, its movements and its sensations. You could notice your breathing or the feeling of your feet against the ground or floor. Notice your muscles. Notice the sports equipment you may be using. Don't try to memorise this list! These are just suggestions of how to cultivate awareness of your body in action. Especially if you feel pain, notice the full body rather than focussing on the pain. Notice those parts of your body that are not in pain. (This is not, of course, a substitute for seeking medical treatment.)

2. WATCH OUT FOR LABELS. From time to time your mind may apply labels to your experience: tough, disastrous, dead easy, painful, scary, a walkover are just a handful of the huge range of labels that the mind can slap on what you are doing. But these labels distract you from what you need to be doing and sabotage your mental flow. So when you notice them, put your attention back on your body, on your feet against the ground, on whatever sports equipment you might be using and so on.

3. NOTICE WHAT'S AROUND YOU. You can notice sounds, movements, colours. You can notice the way the ball turns or spins as it comes towards you or after it leaves you. In golf you have ample opportunity to notice your surroundings, the shade of the grass, the pattern of trees, the people around you and so on.

4. NOTICE RHYTHMS. Notice your rhythms as you run and move. Notice the rhythm of your breathing. Notice the rhythm of other people's movements. Notice the rhythmic sounds of cycling or of tennis. If you are running, notice the rhythmic pattern of trees you may be running past or of the sound of other runners' feet or of road markings. In golf you might notice the rhythm of your footsteps as you walk from one hole to the next.

5. WATCH OUT FOR MENTAL CHATTER. In sports, mental chatter can be bad for performance. Nothing can take us out of the sensation of flow, of effortless action, more quickly than mental chatter. Sometimes you may need to ask yourself what to do next: what club to use in golf, for example. But be suspicious of the tendency of mental chatter to get in the way and to damage your performance. Shift your attention to your body, your surroundings, your breathing or use any other appropriate technique from this section to lure your mind away from its chattering. This helps increase your concentration and your focus and adds greatly to your effectiveness as a sports person.

6. BE NON-JUDGEMENTAL. An accepting, non-judgemental attitude is at the heart of mindfulness. Time spent berating yourself for a mistake you made a second ago is time wasted and, moreover, can put you off your game. According to top sports psychologist Bob Rotella, champion golfer Padraig Harrington decides, as he prepares to hit each shot, that he will accept the outcome, whatever that may be.[21] This act of acceptance helps him to focus on what he is doing and has improved his performance. Acceptance is not defeatism. In sport, you try your heart out but you accept the result. That way doubts and worries are kept from getting in the way of the work that needs to be done. As people who follow the Constructive Living movement in the United States (based on Japanese Morita Therapy, with a large component of mindfulness) would say: run to the edge of the cliff and then stop![22]

7. BREATHING. Awareness of breathing is the great method of mindfulness and is particularly valuable in sports. Before you take that swing in golf or that penalty in football, for instance, checking in with your breathing can relieve the nerves that might otherwise get in the way. Just notice the movement of your body as your breathe, or the air entering your nostrils, or the diaphragm tightening and loosening to the breath. This act alone will take you into a mindful state. Awareness of the out-breath, and of how it seems to push down into the lower

abdomen, is especially helpful according to Felicity Heathcote, who has taught Zen techniques to a wide range of sports people.

8. FUTURE THINKING. In sports, you need to be performing to your best in the present moment. So thinking about the future, whether that is the very near future ('How the heck am I going to beat these guys? I bet they're really going to turn it on in the last fifteen minutes') or the far future ('They'll kill us if we lose!'), gets in the way of this. Future thinking may help from time to time by reminding you of what you want to achieve. However, what absolutely won't help is getting into a string of thoughts about what might happen later in the game. Use the mindfulness techniques in this section to get out of future thinking.

9. GET OUT OF YOUR HEAD. Mindfulness in sports, then, is about being fully present to what you are doing and not allowing your mind to lure you away into fantasies or worries. You do that by getting yourself into the present moment again and again. Right here, right now — that's the motto.

Practice
Use mindfulness techniques in sports and see your performance improve. Experiment until you find the technique that suits your particular sport.

MINDFULNESS IN COUNSELLING, PSYCHOTHERAPY AND MENTAL HEALTH SETTINGS

NOTE: *This section is self-contained and, therefore, repeats some information which already appears in greater detail earlier in this book. Much of the material in this section originally appeared in the author's 'Mindfulness as a Therapeutic Tool' in Éisteach, the journal of the Irish Association for Counselling and Psychotherapy, September 2008. It contains a list of sources at the end for further study. If you are interested in using mindfulness with clients, I would urge you to practise mindfulness yourself by making use of the material in the earlier part of this book. Only by doing that can you assess the point at which to introduce mindfulness practice to clients and the value of that practice for the particular issues brought to the counselling room.*

A case study

Five years ago, Margaret's brothers convinced their mother to cut her out of a promised inheritance: a share in the farm on which they had all grown up. Her mother died the following year and the farm went to her brothers, who sold it with planning permission for a housing development during a time of booming property prices. Her brothers are now rich while Margaret continues to work hard for a modest income.

The injustice of what was done to her took away Margaret's peace of mind. For nearly three years following her mother's death, she thought of little else. She lost sleep, she was distracted and her husband and children grew sick of listening to her talking about 'the farm'.

Then she learned the practice of mindfulness. As she practised, her obsessive thinking about the farm and her brothers began to fall away. She began to notice what was going on around her, to pay attention to what she was doing and to keep more and more of her awareness in the present moment.

Margaret gradually got back her peace of mind, accepted that she had been out-manoeuvred and conned by her brothers and that she could do nothing about it, and got involved again with the lives of her husband and children.

Definition and explanation

What is mindfulness? Earlier in this book I defined mindfulness as 'an intentional and accepting awareness of what I experience right now'. In a handout I give to clients and other interested parties, I explain mindfulness in terms of the process involved:

> Mindfulness involves taking your attention away from the past and future and away from your imagination, and instead becoming aware of what is going on right now. You can do this as you go about your daily life. Notice where you are, what you are doing, what you are seeing and hearing, notice that you are breathing, standing, walking or sitting or lying down.

Your mind will keep drifting out of the present so you need to keep bringing it back. It is bringing your mind back to the present that makes up the practice of mindfulness. Never criticise your mind for drifting away, just bring it back kindly and gently.

Note that mindfulness involves deliberately maintaining awareness about what is going on, whatever that might be. So it doesn't matter that somebody is drilling on the street outside (not from a mindfulness point of view at any rate), that the free spirit in the apartment above you is playing the drums or that your tummy is growling for food. While practising mindfulness, you simply take it all into awareness without getting into a mental drama about it.

So you note that these things are going on and even that you may be annoyed by them, but you don't make speeches to yourself about how they're always digging up the roads for no reason at all, how people should go out and get a job instead of playing drums in an apartment block or how embarrassed you feel when your tummy starts rumbling during the quiet moments in a counselling session.

You simply note the drum, the drill, the tummy sounds, your annoyance and get on with whatever you're doing.

Noticing in a mindful way what reality brings can help the client to adjust to that reality or, where it is useful to do so, take action to bring about change. A polite request to the free spirit upstairs might be worth more than all the revenge fantasies in the world. Very often it is the mental dramas we engage in under pressure that stand in the way of acceptance and appropriate action. Mindfulness frees both clients and ourselves from these mental dramas.

A basic mindfulness exercise

It is important to give clients a basic mindfulness exercise to help them get into the 'mindfulness zone'. I recommend that you introduce the exercise below to your clients and then take them through the exercise once. They can do the run-through with eyes closed or open, but some clients might find it less embarrassing to close their eyes as they go through the exercise with you. Do explain, though, that mindfulness is a practice for daily life and, therefore, with open eyes.

- Begin by noticing your breathing. You don't have to breathe in any particular way. Just notice your breathing. It might help to notice the breath entering your nostrils or your mouth and leaving again. If your mind drifts into imagination, memory or worries as you do this, just bring it back kindly to noticing your breathing.

- Now notice your posture. Are you sitting, standing, walking, lying down? Just notice.

- Notice your hands. Are your fingers bent or straight? What do your hands feel like? Are they warm or cold? Can you feel a breeze against your skin?

- What about your feet? Can you notice how they feel against your shoes or against the ground?

* Notice sounds. What are the nearest sounds you can hear? What are the farthest away sounds you can hear?

* Notice your emotion. Is it pleasant, unpleasant or neutral? Just notice, then back to your breathing.

* Is there a thought in your mind? Just notice, then back to your breathing.

* Now go back to noticing your breathing. Again, if your mind drifts into imagination, memory or worries, just bring it back kindly to noticing your breathing.

This simple exercise can be done briefly. I usually take clients through it in less than a minute. Clients tend to use it as a sort of brief checklist if they find themselves distracted as they go through their day. With this exercise it isn't important to do everything in the right order or even to do everything at all. What is important is getting into a state of intentional present moment awareness.

Do give a copy of this and perhaps some other mindfulness exercises to your clients. If you wish to contact me at *pomorain@ireland.com*, I will be glad to send you a sheet of mindfulness exercises designed for my clients.

Background to mindfulness practice

Clients who give a little time to this exercise can find it very relaxing, but there's more to mindfulness than that. Mindfulness has been used for thousands of years in the Buddhist tradition to sharpen people's awareness of their patterns of behaviour so that they can step outside these patterns. Mindfulness provides an antidote to brooding (which can lead to, or maintain, depression) and helps people to avoid endlessly repeating distressing or unhelpful thoughts, images and mental scenes. This, in turn, helps avoid repeating unhelpful behaviours.

According to Buddhist psychology, we build up patterns of reactions to events. First, we perceive an event which could be something external or which could be a memory or thought. We then have a reaction which is made up of physical, mental and emotional associations with the event. We are swept away by the reaction, sometimes as if in a trance. This process distorts our future perceptions with the result that we are no longer fully aware of the reality around us.

This pattern, as therapists will recognise, has much in common with Cognitive Behavioural Therapy (CBT), which also recognises the capacity of such reactions to interfere with peace of mind and with healthy psychological functioning. Many practitioners of CBT have incorporated mindfulness into their work.

An example of how these reactions might work is this. Let us say it's Saturday morning and I'm angry at the drilling going on down the street. I am having all sorts of hostile and probably quite justified thoughts about the choice somebody made to do work at this time. I cannot settle down to my newspaper. I bang doors. I fantasise about what I would do if I wasn't afraid of the reaction I would get from the yellow-helmeted fellow with the drill. The doorbell rings and there stands a man who has come to install the thousand-channel satellite TV system I thought I wasn't getting until Monday. Suddenly I am delighted and my mind and emotions are swept away by the anticipation of being able to play with my new toy for the weekend. The drilling no longer exists or, if it does, it is no more than the buzzing of a fly outside in the street. I may be wide awake but I am also in a trance.

Mindfulness teaches us and our clients that we spend much of our day in one trance or another, daydreaming, fantasising, remembering, resenting and so on. Mindfulness offers a way to step out of that process and to get into greater harmony with reality. Mindfulness teaches us to spare ourselves the mental drama about the drilling even though the drilling is annoying; all the mental drama does is inflate the annoyance.

I hope this explanation will show readers why it is that Margaret was able to derive such a benefit from mindfulness. The practice of mindfulness helped her to step out of a series of reactions that was ruining her life far more effectively than her brothers' sharp practice had done. What they did was reprehensible, but if there is nothing Margaret can do to reverse it, then she needs a way to get her life back and that is what mindfulness will do.

Practice and research

Note: Most of the applications of mindfulness mentioned below are covered in greater detail earlier in this book.

KABAT-ZINN AND BANGOR. In recent times, the work of Dr Jon Kabat-Zinn at the University of Massachusetts Medical School has given a huge boost to the use of mindfulness in mainstream health settings. His clinic teaches mindfulness and yoga to people suffering chronic pain and stress. His work has enabled patients suffering permanent pain to re-gain control over their lives, though the pain, of course, persists. In addition to helping patients live more satisfactorily with chronic pain, his clinic has achieved significant and sustained reductions in levels of anxiety, in reducing the severity and frequency of panic attacks and in improving the management of psoriasis. Kabat-Zinn has written up his work in an accessible way in his book *Full Catastrophe Living*.[23] Similar work is now being done in hospitals and other health settings in countries across the world and mindfulness is increasingly seen as a mainstream intervention for many conditions.

The uses of mindfulness in western psychology have been studied intensively at the Centre for Mindfulness Research and Practice at Bangor University, Wales. Many counsellors and mental health nurses have undertaken courses at the centre so as to bring mindfulness into their work with clients and patients. Researchers in Wales and elsewhere have found mindfulness to be helpful in reducing the risk of relapse in persons who have had a number of episodes of depression (Segal, Williams and Teasdale, 2002).[24]

DEPRESSION. One model relevant to mindfulness and developed at Bangor suggests that persons with relapsing depression have unwittingly made a link in their minds between low mood, fatigue and negative thoughts, all of which are aspects of the experience of deep depression. At some point following recovery from depression, one of these three aspects will occur again in the normal course of living. The danger for the person who has been seriously depressed before is that he or she will believe the depression is back and will act in ways that bring this about. So a person who wakes up in a low mood may immediately indulge in negative thinking about the supposed return of the depression, stay in bed and, as a result, feel fatigued on finally getting up. All three aspects of deep depression are now present: fatigue, low mood, negative thoughts – an episode of depression lasing weeks or months can all too easily follow. The client who practises mindfulness, this theory suggests, can spot the occurrence of this pattern and can take action, perhaps in conjunction with the therapist, to avoid an episode. This action might include going to bed and getting up at normal times, allowing negative thoughts to pass without engaging with them and exercising to lift the mood (for more, see 'Depression' in the chapter 'Stress and Distress').

I do not maintain that this approach prevents depression from occurring each and every time it is adopted. What it can do is lengthen the periods between depressions and shorten the episodes themselves. These are valuable gains for anyone suffering the pain of depression.

ANXIETY. In my own work, I have found mindfulness to be helpful to people with excessive anxiety and panic attacks. The excessively anxious person can gain a more detached view of his or her fears and can learn to function effectively even as the anxiety is occurring. The client with panic attacks can benefit by maintaining an awareness of what is going on during the panic attack instead of 'awfulising' to himself or herself about it. The aim is to make the panic attack a less frightening event than before so that the client begins to live without avoidance of places and situations that might trigger attacks. Note that the mindfulness approach does not seek to eliminate anxiety or panic attacks but to change the client's relationship to these experiences. This tends to have the effect of reducing levels of anxiety and the severity and frequency of panic attacks. The main aim, however, is to give the client back the freedom of choice which anxiety and panic attacks can so easily take away.

PARENTING. I have also found mindfulness to be of immense benefit to parents who are 'driven demented', as they so often describe it, by boisterous (to put it charitably) children. By practising the basic mindfulness exercise, these parents can gain presence of mind in the face of their antics. Mindfulness gives them a 'mental space' that enables them to avoid having their emotional buttons pressed by very skilful young button-pressers! Mindfulness is especially helpful to parents who think that their upset in the face of provocation will somehow communicate itself to the kids, who will immediately become model citizens. Actually, parental upset equals attention and if that's the only kind of attention on offer, kids will gladly generate upset in order to get more of it. Teach mindfulness to your parenting clients and they will be far more effective in implementing the interventions worked out in the counselling room.

ANGER. Mindfulness practice – again I am talking about the basic mindfulness exercise – can be a boon to the person whose angry outbursts stem from a habit of angry thinking. The mindfulness approach of noting angry thoughts but avoiding engagement with them can bring quick results. I have also found mindfulness to be a blessing for clients who had learned to use anger almost as the normal currency of interaction with a partner. Mindfulness enables the client to see that there are other choices that may work better – again, choices that will be worked out in the counselling room. Where anger is more deep-seated, the effects of mindfulness practice may be more indirect. Nonetheless, mindfulness will help the client to notice physical tensions and anger triggers.

WORK PROBLEMS. The client who is the subject of nasty or bullying treatment at work has a great deal to gain from the practice of mindfulness. Very often there is little the counsellor can do to help with the objective situation. However, workplace bullying and unfair treatment tend to take away the presence of mind that could inoculate the target against the worst effects of what is going on. I find mindfulness practice tends to restore that presence of mind to people bullied at work and this can be a huge boost to morale. It is worth noting that assertiveness techniques require presence of mind in the person trying to use them and, again, mindfulness gives that mental space, that little moment of detachment that allows the target to choose to use an assertiveness technique.

COUPLE COUNSELLING. Mindfulness can help couples in difficulty to spot their own contribution to their conflicts, including damaging conversational styles and a habitually hostile mental approach to the partner. It can help them to realise on the battlefield, so to speak, that it would be appropriate to use an intervention worked out in counselling. In many cases the introduction to mindfulness might need to be done with each individual partner on their own. It can be explained as a technique to enable them to see relationship dynamics more clearly. Mindfulness also helps the counsellor to maintain presence of mind during the conflicts between partners which almost always break out in the counselling room.

THE COUNSELLOR. As a counsellor you probably already practise mindfulness in the counselling room by maintaining awareness both of your client and of your own reactions to your client. Any counsellor who deliberately uses attending skills is using mindfulness even if he or she does not call it that. If you cultivate mindfulness as a counsellor, you give yourself the opportunity to see connections in the client's narrative that you might otherwise miss. Moreover, a mindful reception of what the client is telling you can beneficially alter the client's emotional relationship to the facts behind the story. All this can be done without in any way appearing cold or excessively detached.

A note of caution

The following are a few notes of caution for therapists introducing mindfulness to their work with clients.

MINDFULNESS IS NOT THE ANSWER TO EVERYTHING. It is too easy to over-sell the benefits of mindfulness, especially at a time when its use is becoming more popular and its benefits promoted with great enthusiasm. I have seen the basic mindfulness exercise bring about major benefits in the lives of some clients and make little apparent difference to others. In many of the cases mentioned above, mindfulness did not provide an immediate solution but revealed to the client what he or she needed to work on – in doing so, mindfulness practice performed a valuable service, but it was the beginning and not the end of a solution. It also provided a context in which skilled counselling interventions could be more effective – a person practising mindfulness can more accurately spot distortions in thinking, for instance.

DIFFERENT PEOPLE NEED DIFFERENT 'KINDS' OF MINDFULNESS. People who live in their heads, endlessly analysing their own thoughts, need to be steered towards mindfulness of the external world, of sights, sounds and other people – a difficult task and I am afraid some will never be convinced the world outside their heads might be more important than the one inside. On the other hand, some clients may need to cultivate mindfulness of thoughts and emotions in the same way that members of Recovery Inc. learn to 'spot' unhelpful habits of thinking.

MINDFULNESS IS NOT AN ANAESTHETIC. Mindfulness is sometimes promoted as a means of relaxation and stress reduction. But while mindfulness reduces stress, its main value is in revealing what needs to be done and sometimes what needs to be done is painful. For instance, the person who uses mindfulness during panic attacks – an approach I advocate – can expect to feel emotional distress during the attack. Some clients, if they practise formal mindfulness exercises, such as the body scan, for lengthy periods may find themselves recalling previously hidden and distressing material. Therapists need to be aware of this and so do their clients. In this book I have described what I call 'light mindfulness' with brief exercises that can give practitioners the benefits of mindfulness without the danger of repressed material suddenly surfacing.

MINDFULNESS MAY BE UNHELPFUL FOR SOME PSYCHIATRIC PATIENTS. When the Buddhist teacher and writer Jack Kornfield worked at a state mental hospital in the US, he tried to teach meditation to some of the patients: 'It quickly became obvious that meditation was not what they needed', he wrote later. He found that the patients had little ability to bring a balanced attention to their lives and that most were already lost in their minds: 'If any meditation was useful to them, it would have to be one that was earthy and grounded: yoga, gardening, tai chi, active practices that could connect them to their bodies.'[25] This is not to say that a person who has received psychiatric treatment cannot benefit from mindfulness. It simply means that mental health professionals need to make a judgement as to whether mindfulness would be helpful to a particular patient.

CAUTION CLIENTS ABOUT THE TEMPORARY EUPHORIC EFFECT. Sometimes persons beginning to practise mindfulness experience a beautiful sense of calm and clarity. It does no harm, but it doesn't last. If a client reports that he or she is having this experience it is worth telling them gently that the effect will fade and that there is nothing to be gained from trying to get it back. You may find a similar effect yourself when you start to practise mindfulness – don't spend time chasing it; it will come back now and then but it will not stay.

WHEN INTRODUCING MINDFULNESS, GET THE TIMING RIGHT. As with everything else in counselling, there is little point in introducing mindfulness until the client feels heard and understood. Sometimes it is helpful to introduce mindfulness towards the end of the first session as a technique which might help. At other times it may only become appropriate to introduce mindfulness at a second or subsequent session. And at times it may not be appropriate at all. This is a matter of judgement and of that sense of what it is right to do and when it is right to do it that counsellors gradually develop. See mindfulness as one tool in your armoury, to be used sensitively.

MINDFULNESS OF THE BODY MAY BE TOO DIFFICULT FOLLOWING PHYSICAL ATTACK OR TORTURE. I am indebted to a participant in one of my workshops for the information that persons who have been tortured can find mindfulness of the body or of breathing quite difficult and frightening. In such cases, mindfulness of one's surroundings, of sounds, of colours and of other aspects of external perception may be helpful. A point may come when a gradual exposure to mindfulness of breathing and of the body would be helpful, but this is a matter for skilled judgement.

Having said all the above, I have no doubt that mindfulness is a valuable practice that can do much to enhance our lives and those of our clients.

Further exercises

Earlier I described an exercise from a handout on mindfulness which I give to my clients. There are two other exercises on the handout and you might like to try them out yourself before suggesting them to your client.

The first is to establish what I call 'mindfulness cues'. This involves using habitual behaviours to remind you to practise mindfulness. Choose one or two and then decide that when performing them you will maintain awareness of what you are doing, rather than daydreaming or getting caught up in fears or anxieties. Examples of mindfulness cues include: using the telephone, going up or down stairs or steps, arranging your desk or other workspace, tidying, washing up or taking a shower.

The second is checking in with the breath. As you go through your day, notice your breathing from time to time. All you need to do is notice: you don't have to breathe in any special way. You could notice one or more of the following: is your breathing different now to what it was a few minutes ago? Is it calmer or more laboured? Are you breathing with your chest or your tummy (abdominal breathing is usually more relaxing)? As you breathe, can you feel movement in your diaphragm (between your ribs and your abdomen)? Can you feel the air entering and leaving your nostrils?

And finally (again) ...

If you want to use mindfulness with your clients, begin by using it yourself. Only then can you answer the questions your clients will have.

SOURCES AND REFERENCES FOR COUNSELLORS, PSYCHOTHERAPISTS AND OTHER MENTAL HEALTH WORKERS

Websites

The Institute for Meditation and Psychotherapy
http://www.meditationandpsychotherapy.org/index.html. Click on the 'publications' link on the home page.

Centre for Mindfulness Research and Practice, Bangor University, Wales
http://www.bangor.ac.uk/mindfulness/.

Centre for Mindfulness in Medicine, Health Care and Society (CFM)
http://www.umassmed.edu/cfm/. This is the website of the ground-breaking mindfulness centre run by Dr Jon Kabat-Zinn at the University of Massachusetts Medical School.

Dublin Buddhist Centre
http://www.dublinbuddhistcentre.org/index.html. The centre runs mindfulness courses at various times through the year.

Wildmind
http://www.wildmind.org. Offers mindfulness of breathing and other courses online.

ToDo Institute
http://www.todoinstitute.com. Information on Japanese therapies.

Padraig O'Morain
http://www.padraigomorain.com. Mindfulness resources from the author of this book.

Books

A Path with a Heart by Jack Kornfield (London: Rider, 2002). Covers a broader range than mindfulness and not an easy read in my view, though it contains many interesting meditation exercises.

Buddhist Psychology by Caroline Brazier (London: Robinson, 2003). A general introduction to Buddhist psychology by a psychotherapist.

Mindfulness and Psychotherapy, Christopher K. Germer, Ronald D. Siegel and Paul R. Fulton (eds), (New York and London: The Guildford Press, 2005). An excellent book for any therapist interested in going more deeply into the use of mindfulness with clients.

Full Catastrophe Living by Dr Jon Kabat-Zinn, (New York: Bantam, 1990). A detailed introduction to Kabat-Zinn's pioneering work at the University of Massachusetts Medical School.

Mindfulness-Based Cognitive Therapy for Depression by Z.V. Segal, J.M.G Williams and J.D. Teasdale (New York: Guilford Press, 2002). The main focus of this important book is on preventing relapse into depression.

Calming Your Anxious Mind by Jeffrey Brantley MD (CA: New Harbinger Publications, 2003). Applying mindfulness to anxiety, fear and panic.

NOTES

1. Basic Books, 1995.
2. Fount Paperbacks, 1990.
3. Hyperion, 1994.
4. Rider, 2008.
5. Hodder Mobius, 2001.
6. *Sweet Zen*, Present Perfect Books, 2000.
7. *Reconcilable Differences*, Guilford Press, 2002.
8. Francis Dojun Cook, *How to Raise an Ox*, Wisdom Publications, 2002.
9. Image Books, 1984.
10. *Reclaiming Vitality and Presence: Sensory Awareness as a Practice for Life*, North Atlantic Books, 2007.
11. Dominican Publications, 1987.
12. *Choice Theory*, HarperCollins, 1998.
13. *Mindfulness and Psychotherapy*, Guilford Press, 2005.
14. Caroline Brazier, *Buddhist Psychology*, Constable & Robinson, 2003.
15. *Choice Theory*, HarperCollins, 1998.
16. *A Handbook for Constructive Living*, University of Hawaii Press, 2002.
17. Bantam, 1990.
18. http://www.mind.org.uk.
19. *The Lucifer Effect: Understanding How Good People Turn Evil*, Random House, 2007.
20. Felicity Heathcote, *Peak Performance – Zen and the Sporting Zone*, Wolfhound, 1996.
21. http://www.padraigharrington.com.
22. http://www.todoinstitute.com.
23. Bantam, New York, 1990.
24. Z.V. Segal, J.M.G. Williams and J.D. Teasdale, *Mindfulness-Based Cognitive Therapy for Depression*, Guilford Press, 2002.
25. *A Path with a Heart*, Rider, 2002.

APPENDIX: THE QUICK GUIDE TO MINDFULNESS

In a hurry? This Quick Guide will give you some basic information to help you to start practising mindfulness straight away so that you can begin to enjoy its benefits. If you like the experience, do come back, read the rest of the book and try out the exercises. Skip around if you have a skipping-around sort of mind. If you're a mental health worker, be sure to take a look at the chapter 'Mindfulness in Counselling, Psychotherapy and Mental Health Settings'.

Here we go with the Quick Guide:

WHAT IS MINDFULNESS? Mindfulness is a very old technique that is becoming increasingly popular at the present time. Although it is linked to Buddhism, most of the people who use mindfulness in the West today are not Buddhists. People use mindfulness because they find it reduces stress and gives them a greater sense of control over their lives. Mindfulness helps people to get more enjoyment out of their good times and to handle their bad times better.

HOW DO YOU DO IT? At its simplest, mindfulness means being deliberately aware of what you are doing while you are doing it. This means being aware that you are breathing, walking, driving, running, making a phone call, cooking a meal and so on. When you have thoughts, just notice them and come back to awareness of what you are actually doing. When you are emotional, just notice the emotion – not trying to deepen it and not trying to push it away – and come back to awareness of what you are doing.

IS MINDFULNESS THE SAME AS LIVING IN THE NOW? Yes. When you practise mindfulness, you gently bring yourself back into the present moment every time you notice that you have drifted into the past or into the future. Also, you gently bring yourself back to the present moment whenever you realise that you have wandered off into your imagination. The word 'gently' is important. Never, ever scold yourself for drifting away from awareness. Drifting is what minds do. Accept this fact and gently take your awareness back to the present moment.

CAN I STILL PLAN AND THINK ABOUT THINGS I NEED TO THINK ABOUT? Yes. In fact, mindfulness can be really helpful in planning because it can reduce the chances that you will get lost in a fantasy. You can plan mindfully by being aware that you are planning and by bringing your mind back to what you are doing whenever it drifts off.

ARE THERE SOME QUICK EXERCISES I CAN DO TO HELP ME TO CULTIVATE MINDFULNESS? Yes. Here are three:

---

1. *Get in touch with your senses.* Notice the temperature of your skin. Notice that you are breathing in and out. Notice background sounds around you. Notice your breathing. Do this at intervals during the day — it need only take a minute and you can even do it with your eyes open!

2. *Notice your breathing.* Just notice that you are breathing in and out. Notice the in-breath and the out-breath. When thoughts come into your mind just let them float on by. Do not get involved with them. Simply go back to noticing that you are breathing in and out.

3. *Create mindfulness cues.* Pick some everyday things that you do routinely. Decide that whenever you do them you will be mindful and will be aware that you are doing them. Examples are: using the telephone, going up or down stairs or steps, arranging your desk or other workspace, tidying, washing up, taking a shower.

ARE THERE OTHER MORE INTENSIVE EXERCISES I CAN DO? Yes. If you want to cultivate mindfulness more deeply, try one of these:

AWARENESS OF BREATHING. Sit still. Notice that you are breathing in and out. Notice the in-breath and the out-breath. If you are breathing through your nose, notice the air is colder when entering your nose than when leaving. When thoughts come into your mind just let them float on by. Do not get involved with them. If you like you can just label your thoughts: when you get a thought, just say to yourself 'thought'. Then simply go back to noticing your breathing in and out. If you like, you can count your breaths, counting from one to ten and then back to one again. Do this for ten minutes, once or twice a day.

AWARENESS OF WALKING. Walk along slowly. Notice the feeling of the ground against your feet. Notice your breathing as you walk. Walk in a straight line or a circle or up and down in some place where you will not be interrupted. Again, when thoughts come into your mind just let them float on by. Do not get involved with them. If you like you can just label your thoughts: when you get a thought, just say to yourself 'thought'. When you drift into your imagination bring your mind back to your walking. Do not look at your watch too often. Just be aware that you are walking, of the feel of walking and of your breathing. Do this for twenty minutes once or twice a day.

WHEN DO I START? Right now! Mindfulness and its benefits are available to you whenever you decide to practise awareness. Enjoy it.

NEWSLETTER. If you would like to receive my monthly mindfulness newsletter with reminders of mindfulness practices by email (free of charge), contact me at *pomorain@ireland.com*. For more information on mindfulness, visit www.padraigomorain.com.